Made [D1485445] dy

February 1920

SHIP ALLEY

BY THE SAME AUTHOR

SONGS AND CHANTIES
SAILOR TOWN DAYS
SEA SONGS AND BALLADS
A BOOK OF FAMOUS SHIPS

SHIP ALLEY
(" THE VALIANT SAILOR," KING'S LYNN)

SHIP ALLEY

MORE SAILOR TOWN DAYS

BY

C. FOX SMITH

WITH SIX ILLUSTRATIONS BY
PHIL. W. SMITH

METHUEN & CO. LTD.
36 ESSEX STREET W.C.
LONDON

First Published in 1925

PRINTED IN GREAT BRITAIN

CONTENTS

PARTS of certain chapters in " Ship Alley " have appeared in the " Daily Chronicle," the " Nautical Magazine," and the " White Star Magazine," to the Editors of which periodicals the Author is indebted for permission to reprint ; as also to Captain Sir Acton Blake, K.C.V.O., F. V. Smythe, Esq., and Captain Hutchinson, R.N.R., O.B.E., for their kind assistance regarding Trinity House, Dunbar Wharf, and the "Cospatrick."

LIST OF ILLUSTRATIONS

SHIP ALLEY

PROLOGUE

STREETS have characters, as surely as men and women ; or perhaps it is more truthful to say that they take into themselves by some mysterious process of assimilation the characters of those men and women who most frequent them. And even as humanity—when all minor differences of race and speech are duly allowed for—tends to fall into certain well-defined divisions of type and class, so also there are streets the world over which have a strange inner resemblance underlying their superficial divergences. So, there are of course what every one knows as " mean " streets ; but there are also furtive streets, sinister streets, and evil streets ; sombre streets and cheerful streets ; kindly streets and inhospitable ; pompous streets, smug streets, prim streets ; rakish, devil-may-care streets ; humble, apologetic streets, and pushing, showy, vulgar ones.

Thus in every great city there is a Quality Street (or, as some call it, Vanity Fair), where everything

breathes of leisure, and ease, and all the pleasant
superfluities of life . . . and there is a 'Change Alley,
where men hurry hither and thither with knitted
brows, absorbed and preoccupied by the feverish
pursuit of riches, or haunted by the dread of ruin . . .
and if it be a country town there is a Market Street
or a High Street, where on certain days of the week
red-faced farmers straddle in leather leggings, and
there are gigs and carriers' carts in all the inn yards,
and women with heavy baskets in shabby, rustic
" best " crowding the shops.

And—not in every city, but in every seaport,
great or small—there is Ship Alley : the street that
leads to the sea.

Ship Alley shows many faces to the world. It is
a street of many names—Ship Alley, Paradise
Street, Winchester Street, Wapping Wall, Ratcliff
Highway, Shad Thames, Market Strand, Wharf
Street, Quay Street, Water Street, and a hundred
more besides. It can be sordid or beautiful. It can
be ugly or picturesque. It can be prosperous or
decaying. It can be grey with the greyness of the
North, or glowing with the warmth and colour of the
East and the South.

Sometimes it is a street of little, old-fashioned
houses in a great modern seaport, which look as if
they had somehow got lost there many years ago
and never been able to find their way out. They have
unexpected little green gardens in front of them,

kept trim, as for some reason the gardens of seafaring men mostly are ; and on the doorstep of one
there is a great pink-and-white shell with the lazy
murmur of the tropic seas at its heart, in the parlour
window of another a bottle of gaudy paper flowers
from Singapore.   And at the street corner there is a
church whose graveyard—not yet dug over, and
asphalted, and cindered, and geraniumed, and
lobeliaed into an Open Space—is full of the weathered
tombstones of pilots, and master mariners, and ropemakers, and wharfingers, and barge builders " of
this Parish."

Or else it may be a gloomy cañon between high and
cliff-like warehouses, with projecting cranes dangling
heavy bales perilously over the passer's head, and
an occasional narrow opening through which you
catch an occasional glimpse of a barge sailing lazily
by, or a bustling tug, or the stained funnel of a
steamer . . . or a street of tall Georgian houses
with peeling stucco and blistered doors, and the
words " Seamen's Lodging House " here and there
over a cracked and grimy fanlight.

It leads interminably—slimy and foul when it
rains, gritty with coal dust in dry weather—between
endless rows of small, shabby dwellings and dingy
shops on the one hand, and on the other a dreary
network of railway sidings and forlorn bits of tidal
creek, and derelict cindery cabbage patches that
look as if a gasometer had at some time tried

its hand at gardening and given it up as a bad job.

It straggles along the shore of a famous west-country harbour of the olden time, where artists of the Cornish school paint their pictures in the sail lofts and rigging lofts which remember the old days when a hundred windjammers were driven by stress of weather to anchorage in the Roads. It takes sudden plunges into the blue channel between huddles of odd-shaped cottages, clinging like barnacles to the hull of a ship to the steep sides of the hill, where ling is drying in the sun and nets festoon the walls like some kind of queer leafless growth. It goes between stately houses of forgotten merchant princes . . . by forsaken wharves where grass grows between the cobbles, and the wind pipes mournful ditties in the empty sheds, and all its ships are the ghosts of ships. There are Ship Alleys that smell of sawdust and lumber, of whale oil and nitrates. There are Ship Alleys that have never heard the sound of the tides, the sea coast of Bohemia translated into terms of actuality, where masts and funnels appear surprisingly in the middle of an inland landscape, and great liners berth hundreds of miles from the sea.

And whenever and wherever you shall find it, it is the street of romance. It is the street where men meet from the ends of the earth, men who last gripped hands half a lifetime since and half the world away.

It is the street where strange names are part of the common coin of speech, where all the races of the earth rub shoulders in their continual comings and goings : the street where fact is stranger than fiction, and the wildest yarns are true.

For is not this Ship Alley . . . the same yesterday, to-day, and for ever . . . the street with the sea at the end of it ?

CHAPTER I

SAILORS' INNS

The Sailors' Inn—Fancy and Fact—Parrots and Pieces of Eight—The Comic Sailor—Stage Inns—The Real Sailors' Inn— The " Old Mahogany Bar "—A Tale of Two Oceans—The " China Ship "—The " Ship Aground."

THE sailors' inn of popular fancy is—as fanciful things have, fortunately perhaps, so often a way of being—very far removed from the sailors' inn of sober actuality.

It is, to begin with, of an incredible, nay, an impossible, nauticalness ; so that, should a landsman venture his nose within it, he might almost be excused for feeling a little seasick. No oath uttered there but should have a salty savour. No tobacco should be permissible but the most potent ; and even then it should be by preference not smoked but chewed. There should be an all-pervading odour of rum ; and mere songs should never be sung there, but only " chanties "—pronounced, if you please, " tshahnties." A parrot, needless to say, should be present, a bird full of strange oaths and dark sayings about dead men and pieces of eight ; and a very fair proportion of the patrons of the

6

establishment should lack their full complement of legs or eyes.

That is one brand of imaginary sailors' inn. There are, of course, others—as, for instance, the comic variety, called as a rule by some such name as the " Lobster Pot " or the " Salmon and Shrimp," and frequented by jerseyed beings whose mentality combines the intelligence of a two-year-old child (and backward at that) with the cupidity of a magpie and the low cunning of a Barbary ape. And there is the stage inn, with a capital sea view from all windows, like an eligible boarding establishment—the view, however, being rather frequently obscured by the slow and impressive passings by of strangers of sinister import. In these stage inns it is customary to count one's pieces of eight or inspect one's secret maps in full view of the windows, without taking the obvious precaution of drawing the curtains or shutting the shutters.

Alas for such fond delusions ! These haunts do not exist off the stage or outside the covers of sea yarns. I doubt, indeed, if ever they did. It seems likely enough that, the further back one went into the past, the more evil, sordid, and odoriferous would be the haunts of the sailorman ashore, the less obvious on the face of it the quality of romance.

And yet undoubtedly the sailors' inn to-day has

not the significance that once it had, in times when his daily life was made up of periods of protracted hunger, hardship and toil, punctuated by orgies of drink and lust the more magnificent because of their transiency. Hungry, wet, cold, soaked to the skin for days and weeks upon end, sodden through and through with salt water, eaten with sea boils, he dreamed of the warmth and light and coarse comfort of some Wapping alehouse or Paradise Street drinking den as mediaeval visionaries dreamed of Heaven. He thought of it fighting frozen sails off the pitch of the Horn. He remembered it hauling yards in the weary doldrum weather. He pictured it, yarning of its delights with his shipmates in the golden Tropic dog-watches.

It does not—how should it ?—mean so much to him nowadays. It is not sufficiently remote from him to gain the glamour of distance. His life is on the whole less arduous, less hard, less fraught with danger, and the contrast in proportion all the less striking. He lives at sea as well as—perhaps better than—he does ashore.

It must be admitted, too, that the old sailors' inn had its picturesque qualities—qualities which are sadly lacking in the modern public-house, with its shiny red and green and yellow tiles, its plate-glass windows, its interior gleaming with polished counters and the latest thing in the way of beer engines.

You find them still, these old taverns, in the narrow streets of mouldering coast towns, or by deserted quays where ancient pilots gather to smoke and spit into the harbour and exchange gossip and reminiscence, or squatting in the mud of tidal creeks where the sea is slipping away year by year from the land. There are forlorn inns all shut up and deserted, empty and full of ghosts, like the coaching inns on the Great North Road. There are little inns up steep twisting by-ways in Cornish fishing villages, huddling away from the winds and the winter storms with the characteristic sailor's dislike of too much fresh air when he is separated from his customary element. There are old, leaning, tarred, lapboarded taverns on Thames-side, with their inevitable suggestion of mist and escaped convicts. There are Norfolk inns, bleak, square, uncompromising, made to resist the fiercest nor'-easter that ever came sweeping in from the sea. There are handsome inns for officers and passengers, too, like the old " Dolphin " at Southampton. There are smugglers' inns and wreckers' inns. There are inns for coasting folk and inns for deep-water men. And though in the greater number of them you might sojourn all day and find nothing more exciting than a smell of stale tobacco and staler liquor, yet there is in the sailors' inn of reality a lurking romance—if but a sordid kind of romance—which outruns all the architecture of fancy.

If walls could speak, to use the well-worn figure, surely no bricks and mortar man ever builded could tell more enthralling tales. What yarns would be theirs of courage, of endurance, of brutality, of the eternal terror and wonder and sorrow of the sea! What blendings of the sublime and the degraded, of the spiritual and the material, of the noble and the base! What strange names of the far corners of the seas should be woven into their utterance; and what echoes of forgotten choruses sound through them, faint and far off as the distant thunder of the sea on reefs a world away. . . .

. . . . .

We feasted on dainties and drank of the best,
Thought I, with my friends I am happily blest:
For punch, beer, and brandy they every day did call,
And I was honest Johnny, Johnny pay for all, all, all,
And I was honest Johnny, Johnny pay for all.

They pledged me so warm that in truth I might say
I scarce in a month knew the night from the day.
My hostess I kissed though her husband he was by,
For while my gold and silver lasted, who but I, I, I,
For while my gold and silver lasted who but I?

This life I did lead for a month and a day,
And then all my glory began to decay,
My money was gone, I quite consumed my store,
My hostess told me in a word she would not score, score,
    score,
My hostess told me in a word she would not score.

She frowned like a fury and Kate she was coy,
A kiss or a smile I must no more enjoy,

Nay, if that I called but for a mug of beer,
My hostess she was very deaf and could not hear, hear,
    hear,
My hostess she was very deaf and could not hear.

Now having replenished my stock once again,
My hostess and daughter I vow to refrain
Their company quite and betake myself to a wife,
With whom I hope to live a sober life, life, life,
With whom I hope to live a sober life.

Old Song.

.   .   .   .   .

Wellclose Square is one of those corners of London of which nine out of ten Londoners have never so much as heard, yet which, on the other hand, are probably better known on the water-fronts of Singapore and Vancouver and Wellington than the Houses of Parliament or the dome of Saint Paul's.

It is a queer little survival of old Sailor Town. Round it stand tall houses of that solid Georgian type whose fate it so often seems to be to exchange a once smug respectability for, at best, a down-at-heels shabbiness. Their handsome fanlights are mostly broken, their wide doors, cracked and paintless, exude countless alien *bambini* in various stages of undress, and here and there broad-cheek-boned, bovine women whose ample figures overflow jumpers of barbaric colourings sit suckling their babies on the unwashed doorsteps.

A few trees surrounding the modern school building in the middle of the square where once stood the old Danish church make a pleasant touch of greenness, and there is a quaint little shipboarded place in one corner which looks as if it might have been a barn in days—not very far remote days, either —when there was still a green field or two in this part of the world.

I visited the place not long ago on a sort of disreputable pilgrimage, whose objective was a spot more interesting, if much less respectable, than the identification of the Wellclose Square house once inhabited by that arch-prig and egoist, Thomas Day, the author of " Sandford and Merton."

The place I was looking for was that hostelry of dubious fame once known to seamen the world over as the " Old Mahogany Bar," which, far from being (as I was once told) demolished, still remains, outwardly at least, in many ways very much the same as it used to be in its palmy and unregenerate days.

Its doors open on to a narrow and crooked alley, where lamps project here and there, bearing the legend on their dingy glass, " Seamen's Lodging House." It is the sort of by-way where many a sailorman may well have fallen among thieves, with but a poor chance of any Samaritan's coming to his assistance, in the old wild days when this district about Cable Street and Leman Street bore the well-earned and sinister name of " Tiger Bay." The alley at the opposite corner of the square still bears the

title of the "North-East Passage," and this by analogy
should be the " North-West Passage " ; and in their
way they must have been as difficult to navigate
with safety as their frozen namesakes.

The place swarmed with tigers in human form,
ready to prey upon the newly paid-off sailorman
with his hard-earned cash in his pocket. I have
heard a well-known clipper captain tell how, in his
second-mate days, when he stayed at the Sailors'
Home waiting for a ship, he once saw a man come in
wearing nothing but a soldier's scarlet coat and a
gunny sack round his loins. Another, even more
destitute and certainly more ingenious, had im-
provised for himself a sort of coat-frock by knocking
both ends out of a cask which he had found on some
tradesman's rubbish heap.

Some captains used to try to give their men a
chance of keeping their money by refusing to pay
them off if they turned up drunk. A man would
make a tremendous effort to stand and speak
straight, and hold up his cap to receive his money.
Then perhaps he would clap it on his head, money
and all, so that a cascade of gold and silver would
be scattered over the floor. One man, thinking to
find a safe hiding place, stowed his money in his
boot. He finished a decidedly lurid evening by
going to sleep on the steps of the Sailors' Home,
where he was found in the morning still snoring
happily, minus both his boots and his money.

The front of the "Mahogany Bar" is rather disappointing, for it is neither quaint nor romantic. It has just the ordinary style of mid-Victorian "pub" front, with stucco grapes dangling on it here and there. But inside it is a queer, suggestive rabbit warren of a house, with narrow passages and numberless doors, and the modern front has evidently been a later addition.

At the back of the "bar"—not a mahogany one, but a deal affair where the present occupiers (the Wesleyan Mission) dispense tea and coffee on festive occasions—is a big, galleried room with tawdry gilt and white decorations which belong to the time when it was "Wilson's Music Hall," the heart and centre of the night life of Sailor Town, and one of those places which gave the name of "music hall" a significance in the minds of the respectable which has taken a long time to wear off. Under the distemper on the walls are, I believe, decently concealed frescoes of emphatically nude ladies whose buxom charms were doubtless considered not in keeping with the activities of a Wesleyan Mission.

Old inhabitants of the district still preserve legends of the wonderful "talent" which used to be heard and seen at Wilson's in its heyday. Beautiful dancin'—and some grand singers; there was one gentleman what used to come—George Something-or-other—he was a fine singer, he was, a tip-topper! . . . I wonder who he was, that mythical George

THE OLD " MAHOGANY BAR "

Something-or-other. Some fifth-rate songster, very likely, whose fame never spread beyond the purlieus of Ratcliff Highway; or he may really have been one of the forgotten stars of the days of side-whiskers and pegtop trousers—perhaps even the great George Leybourn himself of " Champagne Charlie " fame.

Another local tradition asserts that the trap-doors which are plainly to be seen in the floor of the music hall had a sinister use of their own in the days of the crimps. When the room was full of drunken sailors, so the story goes, the trap would be opened and the victims dropped into the cellar beneath. I don't know if there is anything in the yarn. The doors may have had no more harmful use than to admit of the passage of barrels of beer. But it is more than possible that at some period of its history the place may have been so used. It was probably a dance hall before it was a music hall, and at that time it is quite likely that shanghai-ing was not unknown there.

The " Mahogany " Bar itself, as I have said, is gone, but some of the old public-house fittings still remain, among them a few heavy mirrors in gilt frames, in whose dimmed and fly-spotted glass fancy might almost call up as in a magic crystal shadowy reflec-tions of the scenes they have witnessed in their day. For indeed it is a queer, ghost-haunted place, this, where a faint musty aroma of bygone clouds of tobacco smoke and of stale liquor still seems to linger, and with it a thin echo of voices roaring out the chorus of some popular song long since lost and forgotten. . . .

.   .   .   .   .

And among the scenes it has witnessed was the final scene of a drama which was at one time common talk wherever seafaring folk gathered together—a drama whose opening acts were played in a setting very far from the drab by-ways of London's sailor town.

It was in the days when the captains of clipper ships used to consider that all was fair in love, war— and tea races. Very slim tricks they used to play upon one another sometimes, if any advantage was to be gained over a rival by doing so ; such as giving another ship's name to put another skipper off his guard, or making ostentatious preparations to anchor, only to make sail again and away as soon as the plunge of the other's mudhook was heard and the rattle of the cable through the hawse-pipe.

A dark night pierced with stars . . . faint airs bringing warm, spicy scents from the islands which loomed through the dusk . . . and three clipper ships anchored in Banca Strait in a dead calm. During the night the wind rose a little, and the captain of one of the ships gave the order to heave the anchor. Everything was to be done as silently as possible. There was to be no shantying.

Stealthily the windlass began to revolve—weary work, for the sailor hates to work without a stave to put heart into him. Then, suddenly, there came the queer, penetrating falsetto of a negro lifting a snatch of a shanty!

Perhaps it was sheer habit, perhaps he had misunderstood the order, perhaps it was sheer insolence —probably the latter, for the nigger was a cheeky nigger, who had given the mate back-chat more than once.

" Shut up there, ye black son of a blister! " said the mate, between his teeth.

Silence for a few seconds—then yet once more came that quavering, plaintive falsetto.

> Sister Susan, my aunt Sue,
> Gwine ter git a home by'm by. . . .

This time the mate said nothing. He jumped and struck—struck with one of the clipper's iron-bark capstan bars. And that nigger had sung his last song. Perhaps the mate had hit harder than he meant to. Or perhaps he had come to the clipper from an American ship, where capstan bars, being made of yellow pine, were not hard enough to break the heads of the sons of Ham.

The mate slipped ashore, no one, except it were

the captain, knew when or how. And the China
Seas swallowed him up for a few years.

There the whole matter might have ended but
for one man. That man was the clipper's cook,
who for some reason or another had it in for the mate,
evidently a man with a knack for making enemies.
And the cook swore that if he waited twenty years
he would bring him to justice in the end.

And now the scene changes from the dark, scented
night among the islands of the China Seas to the
" Old Mahogany Bar "—not twenty, but two years
later.

You may fancy the place crowded as usual—full
of noise, and oaths, and drunken laughter—and
among the crowd a seaman just ashore from a
voyage East. A big fellow, who never talked very
much about his past, he stood there against the bar,
drinking heavily and speaking little. And he didn't
notice a man who worked his way through the crowd,
and stared at him, and stared again, and then
wormed his way again out of the bar and down the
narrow alley into Leman Street.

At the corner, as luck would have it, he ran into
the arms of a policeman.

" There's a man in there," said the cook of the
clipper ship, " you can git him if you like. He killed
a nigger in the China Seas."

The policeman heard his tale. The man was
drunk, but he wasn't drunk enough not to know

what he was saying. It might be some sort of a plant. Still, it was worth chancing.

And when the ex-mate, full to the back teeth, rolled out into Wellclose Square, a hand fell on his shoulder. The two years' old crime had found him out !

.   .   .   .   .

I first saw the " China Ship "—just its name and a glimpse of its upper story windows—from the deck of the old " Harmony " in Hermitage Basin and there was a hint of romance about it that was sufficient to make me want to see more.

I found it at one side of a little triangle of which the rather quaintly named Hermitage Street (in which the " China Ship " stands) forms one side. At close quarters it was, frankly, a little disappointing. It has every appearance of being an old building, but it has had a new front put in quite recently, unlike its neighbour, a " good pull-up for carmen," with a very wooden-looking steed painted on its glass door to advertise the fact, and a bulging, small-paned window which must have been there long before the grim, frowning wall opposite which divides Red Mead Lane from Hermitage Basin.

The past of the place is " wropt in mystery." The only thing in the least Oriental about it is its name ; but that, at any rate, is suggestive enough,

though no one seems to know just how it came
by it.

Was it called after some China trader of John
Company's day, and had it, once upon a time, a
sign displaying a bluff-bowed, apple-cheeked East
Indiaman off Java Head or in some Far-Eastern
harbour ?

Again, was the original " China Ship " an opium
clipper, and had mine host served in one of the fast
brigs and schooners which in the first quarter of the
last century were engaged in that no doubt reprehen-
sible but adventurous and highly lucrative trade ?
Or was she a China tea clipper, and was it the
" Challenger " or " Fiery Cross " or " Sir Lancelot,"
or one of the famous Americans, " Oriental " or
" Sea Serpent " or " Flying Cloud," which figured
on the sign ?

On the other hand, the " China Ship " may have
been a model of a junk or lorcha which served as an
ornament of the bar and an attraction to maritime
custom, either of Chinese workmanship (and if you
want to see what beautiful model makers the Chinese
are, just look at one or two examples of their handi-
work in the South Kensington Museum), or made by
someone who had sailed East in days when it was
still rather a distinction to have done so. Lastly,
it may have been a China Ship simply in the sense
in which a teapot is a China teapot—that is to say,
it may have been made of china—in which case

what golden dreams the very thought of it would arouse in the breasts of collectors !

But which, if any, of these surmises is the right one, no one seems able to tell. The romantic past of the " China Ship," if indeed it ever had one, is lost and forgotten, though this too used to be a warm enough corner of Sailor Town within the memory of man. It is not very many years back that, in Messrs. Hoare's Brewery in St. Katharine's Way, they used to keep handy a rack of boarding pikes and cutlasses, such as were used for defence against pirates in the China Seas, with which to repel incursions of the shore pirates of Wapping.

But all those days are past now. . . . The streets are mean and drab and refuse-littered, and the fine rain of a chill autumn dusk is beginning to fall. Perhaps, after all, it would have been better to have been content with that far glimpse of romance over the high dock wall, with the rigging of the old ship making an appropriate foreground.

.   .   .   .   .

One of the charms of Sailor Town is its continual unexpectedness. You may think you have explored it through and through, and still your rambles seem to bring constantly something new to light—some odd corner, some survival of bygone days, some relic of the past. It is almost as if old buildings stole silently in by night as the ships steal into the docks—often, alas! to vanish as the ships do.

It was in the course of a recent stroll in a part of the waterside which I had expected to draw blank that I chanced to notice a survivor of the old-fashioned type of sailors' inn whose name was as unusual as it was suggestive.

The " Ship Aground," for such is its curious title, is situated in Broad Street, Shadwell, a continuation to the eastward of old Ratcliff Highway, formerly so well provided with taverns that about fifty of them have lost their licences and still left quite a fair allowance. Unlike " Paddy's Goose," whose white swan still stands somewhat ungracefully on the coping of the lads' club which has taken its place, and the " Crooked Billet," another Ratcliff inn whose record goes back to the eighteen-twenties, the " Ship Aground " has retained the appearance of antiquity, and a tablet on the front of the house, recording the fact of its rebuilding late in the eighteenth century, indicates that there must have been an even older structure on the present site.

But it may, and probably does, go back farther still. The name may quite possibly refer to some actual ship which—her seagoing days at an end— served as a habitation and as a temporary hostelry for the people of the Shadwell and Wapping water-front.

There is more than one authenticated instance of this kind, the earliest being perhaps the " Golden Hynde " (ex " Pelican "), in which Drake circumnavigated the world. The old ship ended her days as a none too reputable resort at Deptford, but she was probably moored and not actually aground except at low water.

During the Californian gold rush round the Horn in 1849 and onwards there were many cases of ships deserted by their crews which were converted to all kinds of unexpected uses. Notable among these was the British full-rigged ship " Niantic," whose hull was first used as a warehouse. Afterwards it—or rather she—was burnt out during one of the not infrequent fires which used to break out at intervals during the early days of wooden 'Frisco, and the remains of the hull formed the foundations and cellarage of the " Niantic Hotel."

Years afterwards digging operations in this novel cellar brought to light a number of cases of champagne, which were believed to have lain there since the early days of the gold rush, and these were much sought after at high prices by the surviving " forty-niners " for use at anniversary celebrations.

Many sailormen can remember the time when the rotting timbers of one of these deserted ships were still to be seen under one of the 'Frisco wharves of which they formed a part ; and another vessel—the " Apollo "—was converted into a saloon, her lower forecastle being the scene of many a sailors' sing-song.

But perhaps after all it may be no such history which belongs to the old " Ship Aground." The name may be no more than an obvious sort of allegory—a symbol of the old shellback whose sailing days are over—who, like some old stranded ship on the river mud, sees the busy traffic come and go, with a sigh, a memory, a regret for the days when he too went and came on his lawful occasions to and from the ports of the Seven Seas.

CHAPTER II

OLD STEPNEY CHURCH AND ITS MEMORIES

YOU would hardly expect to find either anything old or anything particularly salty in Stepney nowadays. Ratcliff and Shadwell and Wapping have the genuine waterside savour. But Stepney is plain ugly. You turn aside from Commercial Road at its least attractive spot, and you walk through dreary, sordid, uninteresting streets—and then, suddenly, you come upon a stately old church standing amid surroundings which keep here and there the shadow of a bygone picturesqueness.

This is the old church of Stebonhithe, which stood there by Stepney Green when it *was* green, and perhaps even had geese upon it : long before Queen Anne's Bounty brought into being the new churches of St. George's-in-the-East, and Shadwell, and Limehouse. And there is still a certain air of antiquity about the green, for all it has been turned into a modern recreation ground ; and its public-houses—its " Ships " and " Blue Anchors "—no doubt stand where old taverns bearing the same names stood for centuries past. It must have been more old-world still before the Victorians rebuilt Lady Mico's almshouses ; let us hope they made them much more comfortable than the old ones.

And this old parish church of Stepney may in fact claim to be—on this side of the water at least— the cathedral of dockland. Here lies buried Sir Thomas Spert, builder of the famous " Harry Grâce à Dieu " for King Henry the Eighth, the Comptroller of whose Navy he was, and founder of the Guild of the Trinity, from which the present Trinity House is lineally descended. His gloomy tablet is placed very high up on the north wall of the chancel, and its position, together with the deposit of Stepney grime which liberally coats it, makes it impossible to read the inscription without the aid of a step-ladder. Indeed, for some reason most of the Stepney memorials seem to have been designed for the benefit of a race of giraffes, for they are nearly all so placed as to give anyone studying them a crick in the neck, including one of a ruffed husband and wife with a procession of kneeling sons and daughters.

Another nautical celebrity whose epitaph is to be found here is Rear-Admiral Sir John Leake—not a very promising name, surely, for a sailor, the superstitiously inclined might think. Leake was a Rotherhithe man by birth, and, so his tablet records, was "Commander-in-Chief of her late Majesty Queen Anne's fleet," and "anno 1689, in the 'Dartmouth,' by engaging Kilmore Castle, relieved the city of Londonderry in Ireland, also, anno 1702, with a squadron at Newfoundland, he took and destroyed fifty-one sail of French, together with all their settlements. Anno 1704 he forced the van of the French fleet, at the Malaga engagement; relieved Gibraltar twice, burning and taking thirteen sail of French men-of-war. Likewise, anno 1706, relieved Barcelona, the present Emperor of Germany besieged therein by Philip of Spain, and took ninety sail of corn-ships; the same year taking the cities of Carthagena and Alicant, with the islands of Ivica, Majorca, Sardinia and Minorca." With such a list of achievements it is hardly wonderful that he was known in his day as the "brave and fortunate." But one of the first acts of King George the First after his accession was to dismiss this stout and valiant old sea-dog from all employment under the Crown !

And to the present generation, no doubt, his name means little more than that of "Abraham Rallings Mariner of Wapping," who with his son was buried, so a rough tablet in the north-west corner of the church records, in 1644.

Rallings is a good old seafaring name. In another form it was borne by one John Rawlins, who made a valiant escape from captivity among the Algerines in the seventeenth century. They allowed people more licence in those days as regards orthography; but this Rawlins I think was a Rochester man.

Where did he sail in his day, I wonder, this Abraham Rallings Mariner? Perhaps to the Indies with Drake, perhaps—and more probably—he may have been among the company which went a-venturing to Greenland, as Spitzbergen was then called, in the ships of the Muscovy Company. There were many Wapping and Redriff men in those expeditions, and the vanished " Ship and Whale " inn in Wapping High Street no doubt dated from the days of the Greenland Fishery. It had, probably, a sign like one of those pictures one sees in old accounts of the whale fishery, showing an impossible whale swallowing a ship whole; and very likely it may have been kept by some old retired spectioneer or harpooner, full of strange yarns and stranger oaths.

Outside the church wall at the same point is another stone which is worthy of notice. It records the burial of one " Honist Abraham Zouch Ropemaker of Wappin Wall." I have seen the prefix " Honest " on a tombstone before : there is one in Romsey Abbey. But there is nothing in either case to prove if it is a Christian name or a mere epitaph in praise of the dead.   If the latter, no one could ask for a better ; and all the many-syllabled eulogies which crowd the grandiose memorials of greater men could in the end convey no higher praise. " Honist Abraham Zouch " . . . a man who made ropes honestly !   If he had made them dishonestly he might have grown rich, but his wealth would have carried with it the curses of drowned seamen.

His wife lies beside him, and on the other side of her her second husband.   I have often seen a man and his two wives on one stone ;   very seldom, I think, a woman and two husbands.   She must have been a bit of a feminist born out of due time.

And now to turn to another monument which at first sight one would take to be much older than it really is.   That is the tablet on the wall of the south aisle to the memory of the late Joseph Somes, Esquire.

Very few people nowadays have heard of Joseph Somes, Esquire.   Let us see what the tablet has to say about him.

JOSEPH SOMES ESQUIRE
Member of Parliament for Dartmouth
departed this life June XXV MDCCCXLV
in the LVII year of his age.

By the sedulous application of a powerful mind
he raised himself to the position
of the most extensive shipowner
in this great commercial country.

An unexpected internal malady
brought on by over-exertion in his many duties
removed him from this world
in a few brief hours.

MARIA SOMES
his affectionate widow has erected this tablet
in memory of him
she so dearly loved and valued
She died at Annery North Devon July XXVI MCMXI

" So teach us to number our days that
we may apply our hearts unto wisdom "
Ps. xx. verse XII.

At the foot of the tablet is a representation in
fairly high relief of two frigate-built East Indiamen
lying in the Thames. It is a pity there is no means
of identifying their originals, for they are undoubtedly contemporary portraits. They are certainly
real old-timers, most probably the " Earl of Balcarres " and " Thomas Coutts," or some others of
the famous ships bought by Joseph Somes from
the East India Company at the dispersal of the
latter's fleet in the eighteen-thirties; or possibly
they may be two of the frigate-built Blackwallers
of somewhat later date.

Both ships have their yards cockbilled, for what
reason is not clear, as they seem to be lying well
out in the river. I believe at one time all ships
entering the West India Docks had to cockbill their
yards on account of the narrowness of the entrance,
but that cause would hardly operate here. Possibly

it was an old sign of mourning. It is certainly a
fact that in the ships of Catholic countries it was
customary to cockbill the yards crosswise on Good
Friday. And speaking of this subject recalls that
it is not very long since Spanish ships on that day
used to " keelhaul Judas Iscariot," the betrayer,
our Lord being represented by a sort of Guy Fawkes
effigy which was hoisted up to one yardarm, then
dragged underneath the ship, and so up to the yardarm on the other side.

The orthodox " mourning " for ships is, of course,
a broad band of blue paint round the hull just under
the bulwarks. And in this connexion there is a
tale told about the origin of the Holt Line's familiar
blue funnel.

It appears that one of the early ships belonging
to the line had been bought in consequence of the
death of her last owner. There happened to be a
drum or two of blue paint left over from the mourning band, and as her funnel looked a bit disreputable,
her new proprietor had the economical idea of using
the blue paint to smarten it up a little. Evidently
he was pleased with the effect, for blue the funnels
of the line have been ever since.

The name of Joseph Somes, as the inscription
indicates, was one which bulked very large in the
shipping world of his day. His father was a seafaring man, Captain Samuel F. Somes, who commanded his own ship, the " Samuel and Sarah,"

no doubt so named after the skipper-owner and his wife. The " Samuel and Sarah " was engaged on Government service, and when carrying troops during the war with America in 1809-1813 she was captured by the American frigate " Essex."

Joseph Somes, who brought the firm to the height of its prosperity, began his career, like Green and Wigram, as an " India husband " ; that is to say, he chartered ships to the East India Company, which as a matter of fact did not actually own the greater number of the ships it operated. Owing to the terms of the company's charter, however, it held a monopoly of trade with the East, and consequently the business of an India husband afforded the only field of private enterprise in that quarter of the globe.

When the company's fleet was broken up, Joseph Somes was one of the first to seize the opportunity that was thus offered to private firms. He bought several of its finest ships, paying very high prices for them. For the " Earl of Balcarres " he paid £10,700, and for the " Lowther Castle " £13,950. The " Earl of Balcarres " was a real East Indiaman of the old type depicted by E. W. Cooke, R.A., in many of his etchings. She mounted two tiers of guns, and had on the whole very little to distinguish her from a ship of the line. She was a teak-built vessel from the East India Company's own yard at Bombay, and like most teak ships she lived to a

great age. The " Thomas Coutts," another of
Somes's early purchases, was a Blackwall-built
ship which made very fast passages for those days,
going out once to Bombay in eighty-two days.
The old " Java," the romantic story of whose
figurehead is alluded to in another chapter, also a
teak-built ship, was still afloat as a coal hulk at
Gibraltar in her eightieth year.

Among the later ships belonging to the firm may
be mentioned the " Peeress," which was sunk by
H.M.S. " Canada " in 1887 ; the Sunderland-built
" Merchantman," which foundered in the Bay of
Bengal in the 'eighties ; and the " Star of India,"
sunk in the North Atlantic under the Norwegian
flag when she was over forty years old. The
" Tyburnia " was one of the best-known of the
fleet.   She was a fast ship, and for a time sailed in the
coolie trade.   But she is perhaps most noted for a
comic opera cruise in which she was once engaged
after the Somes family sold her.   The " Europa,"
built at Blackwall in 1851, and the " Eastern
Monarch," a Dundee-built ship, were both burnt.
The latter had troops on board at the time, but
fortunately there was very little loss of life.   Of the
" Canning " (built at Moulmein in 1854) I can find
no record but the name, nor yet of the " Dartmouth "
and " Salisbury."   The " Maria Somes " was in a
cyclone in 1846, during which fourteen of her
battened-down passengers were suffocated.

But the activities of the firm were by no means confined to the Indian and Australian passenger business. At the time of the first publication of Lloyd's Register, in its present form, of which Joseph Somes was one of the promoters, he appears as the owner of more ships than any other private individual, and his ventures were met with in many and varied fields.

Joseph Somes was never a builder. His ships other than those bought from the East India Company were mostly built either at Sunderland, Dundee, or Troon. But he had of course extensive repairing and fitting-out establishments in Poplar, which have been long since swallowed up by extensions to the South-West India Docks.

He always had a large share of Government business, and at one time several of his ships were employed in the conveying of convicts to the various penal settlements—not, perhaps, a particularly attractive line of merchandise ; but somebody had to do it, and Joseph Somes evidently did it well, for he received exceptionally high rates for those of his vessels engaged in this work. Like most of the leading London firms in the first half of the nineteenth century, he owned ships in the South Sea whale-fishery, among these being a Quebec ship, the " Perseverance," built in 1809.

He had also two or three fast clipper ships in the China tea trade. The " Silver Eagle " was built in 1861 by the Portland Ship Company, and she made some very fair passages, her best being 126 days from Shanghai. She disappears from the records in 1869, coming home in that year from Whampoa in 131 days.

The " Leander " was a much better known ship. She was built by Lawrie, of Glasgow, to the designs of Bernard Waymouth, the creator of the " Thermopylae," and although she never proved herself so fast a ship as the latter, she made some excellent runs in her day. One of her best performances was ninety-eight days from Shanghai in 1870. Her name is rather a curious choice on the face of it for anything not meant to find a watery grave ; but as a matter of fact she had a very fortunate career, and lasted well on into the 'nineties, when she was lost in the Indian Ocean with a cargo of salt. Her lines were very fine, and, like so many of the tea clippers, she was, I believe, a very wet ship, especially when loaded with any other cargo than that for which she was intended.

The firm was carried on for some time after its founder's death by his sons, and later became the Merchant Shipping Company, but it has now died out altogether, and the house flag, once so well known in the harbours of the world, is now only to be seen in old pictures and models. In design it was very like that of the other firms which inherited the traditions and much of the business of old

" John Company," showing—in common with the flags of Green, Wigram, and Marshall—the St. George's Cross on a white ground, its distinctive feature being the foul anchor (gold on a blue ground) in the upper canton next the hoist.

The rapid rise of most of the great shipowning firms of the last century is hardly more noteworthy than their complete disappearance. A century ago the name of Joseph Somes was still comparatively unknown. A little more than a half a century ago it was one of the most familiar in the shipping world. And to-day it is—so far as the majority of business folk are concerned—all but forgotten.

CHAPTER III

THE FASCINATION OF CHARTS

Romance in Unexpected Places—The South Sea Waggoner
—Sea Maps and Land Maps—Seller's " English Pilot "—The
Magic of Names—The Thames Estuary—Barley Pickle and
Thief Sand—Mock Beggar Wharf—Who was " Robin Rig ? "

I HAPPENED the other day to be taking a
stroll round a steamer in the Surrey Docks.
She was, to be precise, a Canadian cargo
steamer, as modern as you please, with (one would
have said) precious little of the romance of the sea,
that well-worn term, about her. Nor was she
unloading anything particularly romantic in the
way of merchandise, either ; for it was neither ivory,
apes and peacocks, nor spices of Araby, nor silks of
Ind, nor even furs from the frozen North. It was
in fact Ford cars and Massey-Harris binders.

But the romance of the sea is a strange thing.
It manages to cling to some extent to everything
that floats, save and except possibly bucket dredgers
and mud hoppers.

I had rambled up on to the bridge, where I had
no business at all, unless enjoying the excellent
view of the docks might be called business ; and

from thence I strolled into the chart-room, where I
had less business still. And there, spread out
before me with a pair of dividers beside it, was a
little bit of the romance of the sea—to wit, a chart
of the River Thames and its Approaches !

Now to my thinking a chart is a wonderfully
fascinating thing. True, a modern chart is not the
romantic affair that your old one was. The carto-
grapher of the present day cannot adorn his work
with such flights of fancy as one finds in some of the
old Dutch charts of the long-sought Terra Australis
—the ostriches, the elephants, the rivers pouring
down gold and precious stones. Nor does he
decorate and diversify his ocean with frisking
dolphins and spouting whales and carracks rolling
deep-laden with the treasures of new-found conti-
nents and archipelagos. Even the ornate stars,
like orders of knighthood, which used to indicate
the points of the compass have been swept away.
And gone are those solid slabs of " Treasure Island "
potentialities like the " Buccaneers' Atlas or South
Sea Waggoner " which was published about 1684
by Captain William Hack at the sign of Great
Britain and Ireland, by the New Stairs in
Wapping.

The " Buccaneers' Atlas " is further described on
its title-page as " A Description of the Sea Coasts
in the South Sea of America, viz. from the port of
Acapulco to the straights of Lemaire, it being here

following described at large in 130 particular draughts showing all the Ports, harbours, anchorings, Islands, sands, rocks and daingers in ye distance aforesaid."

The book was compiled from the logs and charts in the possession of the famous buccaneering captain Bartholomew Sharpe, who took part in the sack of Porto Bello and the subsequent march to the Pacific across the isthmus, returning to the West Indies by way of the Horn. During the voyage he fell in with and captured a Spanish ship, the " Rosario," heavily laden with bars of silver ; but mistaking the silver for lead the pirates only took away a few bars, which they melted down for bullets. It was from this ship that there was also taken a " great book of sea maps and charts," and these are probably the foundation of most of the " particular draughts " in the " South Sea Waggoner."

The curious term " waggoner," often applied to old charts, is derived from the name of a famous Dutch hydrographer of the sixteenth century, Waghenaer. The words " map " and " chart " were originally interchangeable, but a sea map as opposed to a land map had become generally known as a chart in English by the sixteenth century or even earlier. And the chart is indeed the seamen's map. The land map disdains the sea, except in the capacity of a mere annexe to terra firma. It indicates with meticulous care mountains, rivers, plains, forests, lakes. But the sea beyond low water mark is, so far as it is concerned, a mere blank sheet, a face without features.

In the chart the positions are reversed. The maker of the sea map takes no account of the land except in so far as it directly concerns the navigator. Its outlines are marked ; so, too, are such excrescences upon its surface, such hills, towers, clumps of trees, and isolated houses, as are visible from the sea. For the rest, the land is blank as the sea in the land map. It is the sea, now, which has its hills and hollows, its closely-written place-names nudging one another for elbow-room , and which, even where names become less frequent, has its rows of figures and its occasional " sand and gravel," " mud," or " rock and stones " to break the monotony.

To return, however, to our " South Sea Waggoner." These are the ideal buccaneer's maps —the sort of thing which one has ever a lingering hope of finding inside the cover of some mouldy old book or serving as padding in one's bedroom slippers. They show little clumps of trees, the " sugar works " of Don This, That, or the Other, the river where ships may load and unload both at high and low water, the mountain where " is a ditch which casteth out brimstone and ebs and flows like the tyde." And the Island of the Holy Ghost, with its solitary dwelling and its few trees—why, it cries aloud for a skull-and-crossbones palimpsest in red, and some crabbed directions for taking bearings from a dead tree and a rock shaped like a man's head, which shall lead you straight to the rusted, iron-bound chests wherein lies the pirates' ghost-guarded hoard.

Ah, well . . . those days are all done with now ! The world is all discovered and charted long ago. Nobody writes " Here much golde " to set young adventurers' pulses a-jigging in days like ours—or, like Cook, notes on the chart of his voyages " nobody knows what." The chart of to-day is a strictly utilitarian affair. It never boasts a decorated title-page like that which adorns John Seller's " English Pilot," printed in 1670 " at the signe of the Marriner's Compasse near Hermitage Stairs in Wapping," and one of the first English volumes of charts ever published. Prior to that date English navigators had been content—or if not content had been compelled by the absence of others—to rely for the most part on Dutch charts, a hydrographical department having been established in that country in connexion with the Dutch East India Company fully a century before the British Admiralty began to think about such a thing.

The title-page of Seller's book is a very imposing affair. It is surrounded by figures of " England's Famous Discoverers "—Sir Francis Drake, Mr.

Thomas " Candish " (Cavendish, of course, is meant), Captain " Davies," Sir Walter Rawleigh, Sir Hugh Willoughby, and Captain John Smith, the latter engaged in studying a chart. In the background are to be seen other unnamed worthies holding up globes and dividers and " shooting the sun " with a sort of primitive quadrant known as a " cross staff." At the foot of the page appear views of London River and of what may be Gravesend or the Downs. In the corner of the latter picture are seated venerable gentlemen, completely unclad but for, in one case, a crown, and holding large urns from which pour copious streams of water. Possibly the gentleman with the crown is intended to represent Father Thames, since his urn is yielding ships as well as water. The other is presumably Old Ocean, or Father Neptune, or perhaps that watery celebrity Davy Jones !

No ! our charts have no such adornments nowadays. Their romance must be sought for elsewhere. But it is there all the same.

There is colour in a chart, read aright. There is atmosphere in a chart—such colour, such atmosphere are there as one does find not seldom where no literary intention is present. I have read somewhere about a man who found all the food his fancy desired in catalogues—seedsmen's catalogues, jewellers' catalogues, catalogues of china, of fabrics, of books. And assuredly there is a wonderful deal of romance in sailing lists, and advertisements of ships for sale—and in charts.

Their names are as old as old England. They have been, perhaps, unchanged since long before Drake's day, before Cabot's day. They were part of the common speech of fisherman and smuggler and coastwise trader long before ever a chart was printed. The great liner of to-day threads her unerring way amid deeps and shoals whose names are the same as they were when the little full-riggers bore bravely up for Liverpool or Bristol or the Nore, just as you may see them on the yellowed old charts of a century and more ago.

There are lovely names, stately names, grim names, grotesque names : names which seem to echo the thunder of the surf on rocky ridges, names which resound with the long roll and hiss of the tide on flat and sandbank, names which owe their origin to ancient legend and tradition, and to maritime disasters of days long gone by. And in all there lingers in more or less degree the wonder and the mystery of the sea.

And of all the charts there be I am not sure that of the River Thames and its Approaches is not one of the most fascinating.

Who can give the real origin of "Kentish Knock"? What bachelor gave his name to " Bachelor Spit " ? The " Quern " is an evident simile. But why " Pudding Pan " ? And what Spaniard, unless it were a captive, could have given long ago a name to a sandbank off the Kentish shore ? " Long Sand " is simple enough, and so are " Fisherman's Gat " and "Black Deep." Has the "Girdlers" any connexion with the Worshipful Company of Girdlers?

The Goodwins are so called, according to Mr. Kipling, from some legendary association with the great Earl Godwin. And the " Gallopers," out towards the " Lowlands Low " of song and story, have probably nothing to do with horses, even white horses. A shoal very frequently takes a semi-circular or double-pointed form in consequence of the action of the tides, and a fancied resemblance to a pair of callipers was very likely the origin of the name, which would then be easily corrupted into " Gallopers." The fact that there is actually a " Calliper " sand shown on the chart of the Goodwins seems to bear out the theory.

Turning east from the Thames Estuary the names grow stranger still : Inner and Outer Gabbard, Bob Hall's Sand, Barley Pickle, The Would, Leman Bank, Kettle Bottom. And the sands of the Wash have some of the queerest and the most picturesque of all.

Here " Thief Sand " calls to mind the occasion when the treacherous sands robbed a king of his treasure. There the " Woolpack " recalls the reef of Norman's Woe whose

> white and fleecy waves
> Looked soft as carded wool. . . .

And there again the " Mare's Tail " conjures up a vivid picture of a shoal in windy weather with the tide just making, and throwing up a tossing plume of foam among the racing white caps.   Then there are " Seal Sand," and the " Bull Dog," and " Vinegar Middle," and " The Trap," and on old charts " Roger " and " Peter Black."

A chart bearing the name " W. Heather " and the date 1804 shows that the approaches to the port of Liverpool have altered very little so far as names are concerned during the last century and more.

There are to be seen Taylor's Bank, Great Burbo Bank (was " Burbo " a person, I wonder ?), Brazil Bank, Hilbre Swash (the equivalent of the Thames " swatch "), and Mad Wharf, a truly suggestive name which one hopes is not a misprint for " Mud " ! It is almost a pity that so quaint a name as " Red Noses " should have dropped out of recent charts. It used to be applied to a part of the long shoal on the New Brighton shore known as " Mock Beggar Wharf."

This " Mock Beggar Wharf " provides a very interesting problem for the student of derivations. It has, of course, its counterpart ashore in the shape of " Mock Beggar Hall " ; but what the term stands for, either by land or sea, no one seems to be able definitely to say.   There is, I believe, a reference to " Mock Beggar Hall " somewhere in Shakespeare.

Possibly it might mean a place where a beggar who expected alms would find himself " sold " ; and similarly " Mock Beggar Wharf " may by a kind of analogy be taken to signify a place where the sea vagrant, thinking to find a safe anchorage, would find himself equally taken in.

" Horse Channel " and " Horse Sand " are names very often found on charts, though their origin is obscure. Another frequently met with, " New Come " Sand or Knoll, probably indicates a sand-bank which had been recently formed by tidal action or by deposits over a sunken wreck at the time the chart was made.

But who shall explain " Cockspeck," near Walney Island ? What unknown " Harry Furlow " handed down his name to posterity in connexion with a rock near Holyhead ? Who was " Robin Rig," and why should he have a bank in the Firth of Solway ? And whence came " The Kish " and " Helly Hunter," over on the Irish shore ? . . . No one can say—least of all, perhaps, the pilots who know them, as pilots have known them for generations, as well as their own hands, and never think of asking.

CHAPTER IV

CHANGING THAMES-SIDE

The Passing of Centre Pond—The Harbour Master's House—
St. Magnus the Martyr—The Fresh Wharf.

EVERYWHERE in London of to-day change
is at work.

It is the same in all those different little
Londons which make up London's whole—in the
West End, in the City, in Suburbia. It eats up
streets, it devours centuries-old landmarks, as it
were, in a night. It lays flat ancient graveyards
and the churches that once stood in them. It wipes
out green fields and pleasant woods, and hides what
once were rippling brooks, where minnows flashed
in the shallows, in noisome culverts far from the
light of day.

So, too, is it in still another London—that
strange, aloof, amphibious London which is the
London of the seafarer. There, also, change is
continually busy, taking for its prey here an old
leaning, galleried building which has stood since the
Stuarts reigned, there a flight of worn and hollowed
steps which the tides have wetted twice daily

47

since the time of the Tudors, there an old sail-loft which goes back to the days of the Royal Dockyard at Blackwall. And now—even as shady Wych Street has passed, even as fashionable Regent Street is passing—so also are Quebec Dock and Canada Pond and Centre Pond to pass away at the dictate of progress.

It is no great matter, perhaps, the substitution of one large dock for three smaller ones, which are, no doubt, inconvenient, wasteful of space, and out of date. It means the disappearance of nothing of any architectural or historic importance— nothing but a few wharf-sheds and a little footbridge or two (indifferently ugly in themselves), a few green and water-worn piles, a few wharves which have been for generations of sailormen the first solid ground their unaccustomed feet had touched for many weary and perilous months, a few old bollards to which in their day hundreds of ships have made fast during their brief sojournings in port, a few stretches of dull and littered water, which have mirrored in their time some of the proudest and fairest ships man ever builded to serve his needs by sea.

And yet one may be permitted the indulgence of a sentimental sigh over their passing. They have a certain quiet comfort, a homely charm of their own, these odd nooks and corners of the old Surrey Docks, which one misses somehow in the big modern ones.

They are the ship's wayside inns ; the others are her modern hotels—magnificent but unhomelike. These are leisurely seeming places, when things are not over busy ; and when the crews are all ashore in Sailor Town, and the stevedores' men have finished work for the day, one might fancy the ships yarning away among themselves of an evening happily enough, and telling their tall tales of the Roaring Forties for the benefit of the lighters and the tugboats and the London barges.

Yes, they will take their memories with them for some of us, these undistinguished stretches of prisoned river water—memories of old ships we have seen there, with the sea-wonder upon them, and the sunset glory upon their spars. They come still, the old windjammers, to such corners of the docks as these, working out their last years in alien bondage, who once were queens of the sea. But their visits are few and far between. Soon, it may be, the last of them will be gone, and a new genera-tion of ships will know Centre Pond no more.

. . . . .

One of the few remaining bits of old Limehouse which has long been marked down for destruction is the fine Queen Anne house in Narrow Street which was formerly the official residence of the Harbour Master of the Port of London. I hardly know why its doom has been pronounced. Its structure still looks sound, though it is dismal, grimy, and deserted enough, in all conscience, with its gaping windows, its crazy shutters, its rusted balconies, and its door panels chalked over with meaningless obscenities.

The old house, with the barge-builders' yard close by, and a few houses as old as or older than itself on either side, is one of the very few remnants of the old water-front. It has its own steps leading to the river at the back, and its wide, shallow bow windows, which still nightly flash back the sunsets from their blind panes like the ghosts of long-dead fires, must command a glorious view up and down the river. How many changes they have seen, watching through the centuries the pageant of London River : what ships, what vanished commerce, what strange and forgotten cargoes ! East Indiaman and West Indiaman, tea clipper and wool clipper, Geordie brig and Sunderland billyboy, Dutch eel-boat and French lugger—the old house has seen them come and go and pass away for ever. And soon it too will go, with its empty, cobwebbed rooms full of the ghosts of old yarns and vanished hospitality, and derricks will rattle and grind out their unremembering clamour on the ground where it stood.

.   .   .   .   .

The narrow strip of waterside which lies in front

THE HARBOUR MASTER'S HOUSE AND "GRAPES" INN, LIMEHOUSE

of the much-discussed skyscraper soon to obscure altogether the view of St. Magnus the Martyr Church from the river side is one of many interesting associations in itself, quite apart from the church and its ancient history.

St. Magnus Church is a lovely little building, whose graceful spire is one of Wren's masterpieces. There has been a church on the site as long as there has been a London Bridge, probably; there are records of one as far back as the fourteenth century, and the chapel which stood on the old bridge was a sort of chapel-of-ease of St. Magnus. But the old church was of course destroyed at the time of the Great Fire and rebuilt from Wren's design. It can never have been a very well-lighted building, and now its dim religious light bids fair to become darkness visible when its towering new neighbour is completed. I wonder how its few plane trees and carefully tended bushes will fare at the bottom of that tall well of yellow brick. They have made a pleasant green corner for many years.

Beneath the projecting clock of St. Magnus—the gift of an eighteenth-century City merchant who had got into a scrape as a boy through loitering by the bridge, ignorant of the flight of time—and the archway which forms a sort of vestibule to the church, was at one time the way which gave access to the steps leading up to Old London Bridge. About the middle of the eighteenth century the path was pronounced too narrow for the amount of foot traffic which passed along it, and the present way had to be made by opening up some of the arches under the church spire. To the left a narrow alley led alongside the river as far as Billingsgate, with shops on either side, which has of course long since disappeared, though the approach to it is still lighted by the City authorities. The quaintly named "Duckfoot Lane" above the bridge is probably a part of the same pathway, which no doubt at one time meandered all along the water-side, much as does the Market Strand at Falmouth.

To the right of St. Magnus Church, and directly in front of the new building, is a narrow wharf where there may generally be seen a coasting or small continental steamer loading or discharging, with perhaps a brown-sailed barge or two to lend its touch of picturesqueness. Its official name is the Fresh Wharf; and, twenty or thirty years ago, the generation of errand boys then leaning over the parapet of the bridge, and watching the gulls and the shipping and the old wrinkling river, as no doubt they have leaned and will always lean as long as there is a parapet to lean on or a river to watch, had a very different scene to look at.

But why, first of all, "Fresh"? That is just the question. There wasn't anything particularly Fresh to be seen when I visited the place. I saw parts of machinery there, and I saw what looked like tea chests, and I saw cases of condensed milk, and I saw huge bales of the wastest-looking waste paper I ever saw in my life being lowered into the hold of a tramp steamer from the Baltic. But nothing which could in the smallest degree be termed Fresh. Nobody seems to be able to offer any explanation. The average Londoner is characteristically incurious, and even if he bears a legend in gilt letters on his cap he seems content without knowing what it means.

The Fresh Wharf may, however, owe its name to the fact that it was in days gone by the headquarters of the little fruit schooners which—before the era of special fruit steamers and cold storage vessels—used to provide London with its few and occasional oranges. They were stout, seaworthy little vessels of from two to three hundred tons—topsail schooners, which could make nine or ten knots in good weather. They used to run to and fro between London and the Azores as long as the orange season lasted; then between seasons they would take a trip over to Newfoundland with salt, returning with a cargo of salt fish for one of the Roman Catholic countries of the Mediterranean seaboard. Next they would load figs, or currants, or olives, at Zante, or Corfu, or Lemnos, or one of the lesser Ægean islands—and so back to the Fresh Wharf in time to load a general cargo and sail for

Ponte Delgado in time for the opening of the Azores fruit season.

A clean little trade—a pleasant little trade—which has become, like many another such, within the memory of one generation as extinct as the galleys of Tyre.

CHAPTER V

THE SEA COOK

Old Slush—Burgoo and Dog's Body—Deep-Sea Fish—Viggy Duff—A Sea Cook's Story.

NOT long ago I climbed many flights of stairs to the top story of the Sailors' Home in Well Street, and there saw a white-capped *chef* instructing a class of budding sea cooks in the mysteries of preparing food for cabin and forecastle. They were learning to make Irish stew and rissoles and a number of other things as familiar to the landsman as to the sailor; and they were also learning to make yeast, which is probably an accomplishment few land cooks possess.

There is perhaps no department of sea life in which recent years have seen so complete a change as in this matter of food. Gone—or all but gone—are the old days of " hard tack " and " hashy gashy," of the time-honoured Liverpool pantile, ancient and weevily, of the salt junk from which the facetious shellback was wont to carve models in those bygone times. And gone—or all but gone—is the sea cook of tradition, whose evil deeds live in many a sailors' song and story.

The profession, if one may term it so, of the sea cook is one which seems to have been regarded from the earliest times with a decided contempt by the rest of the seafaring community. The generic names—and there are many of them—applied to the ship's culinary expert are (or rather were) nearly always fraught with some measure of opprobrium. " Old Slush " and " Grub-spoiler " speak for themselves ; and while one has often heard the phrase " kitchen physic " used as a synonym for " good food and plenty of it," it is safe to surmise that the title " doctor " sometimes conferred on the ship's cook has more reference to the nastiness than to the wholesomeness of his concoctions.

The cook is the seagoing equivalent of the mother-in-law. He is the perpetual butt of the shellback's ridicule or abuse. Take, for example, the old furling shanty of " Paddy Doyle's Boots," which expresses in a few words the characteristic attitude of the old type of sailorman towards the occupant of the galley.

> We'll all throw dirt at the coo-ook,
> And pay Paddy Doyle for his boots. . . .

And what greater nautical insult could be conceived than the term (accompanied, of course, by the

appropriate and sanguinary adjectives) " son of a
sea cook " ?

It may as well be admitted at once that in very
many, perhaps in the majority of cases, the stigma
was far from undeserved. To-day, fortunately, the
Board of Trade regulations provide for some
measure of qualification for the rating of cook in
foreign-going ships, so that he must at all events
have a nodding acquaintance with the duties he
undertakes. But in the old days he very often had
none at all.

A man desiring to " work " (save the mark !) his
passage from one port to another, who was not a
good enough seaman to sign on as A.B., and disliked
the idea of the hard work and poor pay of an
ordinary seaman, might often contrive to pass
himself off as a cook. The job was not without its
attractions, especially to a man of the " skrim-
shanking " type. It was an " idler's " berth for
one thing. The " idlers " in a windjammer were,
technically, those who as a rule had the night " in,"
and did not stand watch and watch like the rest.
Often they were among the hardest workers in the
ship's company : " Sails " and " Chips," for
instance, were " idlers." But at night they only
had to tumble up when " all hands " were called.
The cook had his allotted station in such operations
as tacking or wearing ship. His business was
usually to attend to the foresheet. But as a rule

his nights were undisturbed. And in addition he had the advantage of being able to provide for his own inner man better than the rest of the crew.

And once he had got his job, he might not know a saucepan from a kettle, but the unfortunate crew would have to put up with his experiments for the rest of the passage, and, with the best grace they could, endure his raw or burned meat, his greasy stews, his leathery bread, and his sodden duff. It was a case of " grin and abide " ; or, if they didn't grin, abide at least they must. They had no real remedy. To take the obvious course of heaving his messes at their perpetrator's head was liable to get the aggrieved party into as much disfavour as the cook himself, or even more. Complaints about food seldom got a very sympathetic hearing.

The usual thing in extreme cases was for the whole watch to commit their food untasted to the deep, choosing for the ceremony a moment when the skipper could not fail to witness it. He would then be compelled to admit that the grievance was a genuine one, since hungry men do not go without a meal unless for good and sufficient reason.

But even so there was not much to be gained. Getting the cook sent for'ard might satisfy the desire for vengeance on the " grub-spoiler," but it didn't help much in other ways. Cooks are scarce in mid-ocean—unless, indeed, sea cooks, like other sailormen, inhabit the bodies of sea-birds after death, in which case some late lamented " Slushy " might be flying with melancholy cries after the latest bucketful of galley slops. And the efforts of an amateur recruited from the crew might prove no better—possibly even worse—than those of the dethroned king of the galley.

Add to the deficiencies of the cook the fact that the material at his disposal was often as unpromising as it well could be, and it is hardly to be wondered that those who could wangle such things were glad to supplement their official whack with queer-sounding and queerer-tasting compounds such as probably the modern sailor has never heard of—such dainties as dandy-funk, cracker-hash, dog's body, and burgoo. Burgoo and dog's body were simply euphemisms for cabin scraps ; cracker-hash was made of hard tack and bits of salt junk or pork baked together ; and dandy-funk was also hard tack, in this case pounded very fine with a belaying pin or some similar implement, and mixed into a sort of paste with jam or treacle, the whole being then baked in the galley stove if the cook happened to be in an obliging mood.

Deep-sea fishing also provided a variety from the daily bill of fare of which the sailor was glad to avail himself, though perhaps it was really the sport rather than the fish that he did it for. The deep-sea fish, such as bonito and albacore, are really rather tasteless and sodden things, not worth eating unless nothing better is to be had ; and flying fish are about as bony and unsatisfying a diet as sparrow pie. As for sharks, whatever John Chinaman may think about a shark's fins as a delicacy, the shell-back would have to be very hungry indeed before he would eat any portion of that detested monster.

It was perhaps the sameness rather than the badness of food in a windjammer which was its worst point. Yet the queer thing is that the old sailor—conservative in this as in all things—strongly resented any attempt to interfere with his food. You might try to make his diet more attractive and varied if you chose. He didn't mind. But he had got to have his " viggy duff " on the proper day, or else the fat was in the fire ! " These 'ere calavances and such are all very well. *But where's my duff ?* "

The windjammer cook was not always the sea cook of tradition. Sometimes he could cook, and sometimes he was a seamen as well.

I dropped across one such not long ago in a sailing vessel in the Surrey Docks. He was a Norwegian, one of the fair, stocky type, with eyes the colour of ice, or of the cold northern sky. His life had been a regular saga of varied experience and adventure. He had been in a sealing schooner, for one thing, that used to raid the rookeries of the South Shetlands and the rest of the bleak archi-pelagos of the Southern Ocean. A wonderfully weatherly little ship . . . she could up anchor and away the minute the smoke of a gunboat came over the horizon. She belonged to a German, but she was registered in Chile so as to be able to use the Chilean ports without paying so much in harbour dues. Sometimes they took as many as two thousand seal in the season, and at ten dollars a skin or thereabouts it was a good paying game.

After that he put in a year or more whaling in the Antarctic . . . a nice life, too, and there was money in it all right. They worked on shares, as has been the immemorial custom of whalers the world over, and if you didn't turn out when a whale was sighted, you missed so much of your share. Often he had turned out in his watch below so sleepy that he had held his eyes open with his fingers. . . . But it was a fine life, the whaling ! No dirt with it, either : there was a steamer to do all the cutting in and boiling down. It was right whales they hunted mostly, right whales and finbacks. Those are the whales that don't sink when they are killed. You would just leave them floating with a flag in their backs for the steamer to come along and pick them up.

Well, he got tired of that, and next he was on an estancia, a sheep farm, in the Falklands. He had a good job with a rigger too when there was a ship came in to refit, and he might have settled down there for life only the Port Stanley riggers cut their

own throats with charging the ships too much.
After a while they all had orders not to put in at the
Falklands if they had got knocked about off Cape
Stiff, so long as they could make shift to hobble up
to Montevideo.

So that finished that—and here he was at sea
again, peeling potatoes in the galley of a Baltic
barque. He didn't care about going in steamers—
too dirty—too much messing about in port. You
need a lot of money for that—more than sailors
get !

It is a far cry from the tiny, cramped galley of
the old windjammer to the up-to-date affair provided
in some of the big cargo boats : but it is farther
still from the cooking arrangements of the old
sailing passenger packet to those of the latest
liner.

The first-class passengers in the Liverpool-
Australia clippers seem to have done themselves
tolerably well, to judge by some of the bills of fare :
but I wonder what even the third-class passenger of
to-day would say to a diet provided for the second-
class cabin in the eighteen-fifties, when breakfast was
coffee, biscuits and butter one day, butter, biscuits
and coffee the next, and biscuits, coffee and butter
the third ? Dinner included such dainties as pea
soup, preserved potatoes and salt junk, and plum
duff. And tea or supper consisted of one uniform
monotone of tea, biscuits and butter.

Even so late as the eighteen-seventies, one of Green's crack passenger ships carried the modest kitchen staff of two cooks, a baker and a butcher and their respective mates. By way of contrast, let us glance at the first-class galley equipment of a modern liner, with its three hundred pans, its forty boilers, its electrically driven spits, bacon-slicers and coffee-grinders, its salamanders and refrigerators, its seventy cooks, its fourteen bakers, its three confectioners, and its thirteen butchers (a " butcher's dozen," evidently)—to say nothing of the Hebrew cook whose special business it is to prepare " kosher " meals for the Jewish passengers.

Shades of " Old Slush " and " the harness cask " . . . what a change is here !

CHAPTER VI

CURIOS

Skrimshawing—A Queer Yarn—The Beginning of an Adventure.

I SUPPOSE one of the indirect consequences of the modern short voyage will be a decrease in the number of these odd little toys and trifles the making of which beguiled so large a proportion of the old-time sailorman's scanty leisure. The steamboat seaman will still, no doubt, buy bottled flowers in Singapore, and rainbow-tinted shells in Manila, and what he calls "coral" in the South Seas, and stuffed sunfishes in Colombo ; but he will buy them as any traveller might buy them. And the real nautical curiosity will become as extinct as the type of sailor who made it, surviving only in the families with a seafaring tradition, and finding its way ultimately, dusty and neglected, into the odd corners of Hebrew junk stores.

The old shellback was an inveterate curio collector. He stuffed his chest with all sorts of oddments for the adornment of his home—if he had one ; if he hadn't, it was all the same. He scattered his trophies to the winds as he did his pay, and started on a fresh lot next voyage, just as some birds make nests for the sheer pleasure of making them.

He dried the feet of albatrosses for tobacco pouches. He made himself walking-sticks of the backbones of sharks—which he never used. He made fancy shackles for his chest—and pawned it before he went to sea again. He made little mats of sennet. I wonder how many of the next generation will know how to make sennet, let alone make mats of it.

And it was the whaleman who excelled all others in the production of all kinds of maritime bric-à-brac, or, as he called it, " skrimshawing " or " skrimshandering." Generally with no tool but his jack-knife, he would make all sorts of wonderful devices of whalebone, decorating them with pricked-in pictures of whaling scenes and the like. He had abundant leisure, for the whaler carried so large a ship's company that his watch below was not often interrupted |except when whales were in sight.

That was a strange tale I heard one night on the old Outer Wharf at Victoria—a red glow of evening still lingering over the hills of Vancouver Island, a faint flush on the peaks of the mainland, and a young moon hanging up above the sunset. Star after pale star crept up into the clear blue. A

5

light had just begun to gleam in the rigging of the sailing ship lying at anchor in the Roads, and the beacon on Brotchie Ledge winked steadily out and in, out and in.

The tide was full. Outside, there was a white crest or two flashing; but in the shadow of the wharf the water was dark and silent, but for the sort of running whisper it kept up between the side of the Holt liner and the worm-eaten piles. The grinding of the winches was dumb, and the gaunt outline of the double derricks stood up gallowslike and grim against the faint flush in the western sky.

The little ship that goes up and down the coast with barrels of whale oil lay so much in the shadow of the Blue Funnel vessel that at first you did not notice she was there at all. She also was dark and quiet, for she had just come in that Sunday morning from a cruise to the Queen Charlotte Islands, and the crew were all ashore except the watchman, who was sitting eating his supper on a closed hatch and talking to the ship's cat.

That little ship is an old acquaintance of mine. She started life as a fish carrier in the North Sea, and she still keeps her old sturdy British look, her air of cheerful acceptance of a hard, rough, and little rewarded life, much like that of the average old-time sailorman.

The watchman finished his supper and gave the bones to the cat.

" Ut's a good cat, that one," he observed ;
" ut'll ate bread. Ut's not every cat'll ate bread."

That started the conversation ; and presently I
was sitting on the hatch coaming with the watchman
and the good cat that would eat bread, while the
latter grumbled to herself over the supper bones
and the former worked away diligently at some
white object he held in his hand.

" You couldn't buy the like o' that for money,"
he said, pausing in his work to hold the thing out
at arm's length, surveying it the while with cocked
head and a craftsman's pride. " I'm doin' ut for
a bit of a present for the Old Man's wife. She's a
very good friend to us sailormen."

I looked at the mysterious object with interest.
It reminded one of Othere the old sea captain in
Longfellow's poem, though, to be sure, neither
Othere nor King Alfred had ever heard of Victoria
or the Pacific Ocean, or, for the matter of that,
of a liddle place called Tullane in County Carlow,
where the watchman, so I learned, had been born
an' rared.

" Ut's a sperm whale's tooth," he explained.
" Them sperm whales is the only whales that has
any teeth at all. And I'm doin' the picture on it
wid a needle an' ink—tattooin' it. I have copied
it from a newspaper."

The picture—it was some kind of allegorical
subject, England and America weeping in each

other's arms over the lost " Titanic," I think—was
really very good, and it must have cost a great deal
of patience and perseverance. Indeed, the watchman said it had already taken up several weeks
of his leisure, and was likely to take as many more
yet.

" Thim whalin' stations up the coast was great
places in the old days," he continued, " for gettin'
all sorts o' quare things from. Lashin's of curios,
Indian stuff and the like, not to mention whales'
teeth an' ear dhrums as many as you cared to pick
up. A whale's ear dhrum, now, an' it tattooed, is
a very elegant curio. But thim places is changed
entirely, what with the tourists and the Americans,
and the steamboats callin' regular. There's not so
many quare things in it now.

" Why, I remember up in the Queen Charlotte
Islands twenty or thirty years back, there was old
chairs an' tables, and old ship's lanterns, and cabin
tables all in teak, and sextants and charts, an' the
Lord knows what besides, in the traders' little
cabins up there, the way you'd think the Ark or the
Spanish Armada had stuck somewhere in those
parts an' it sailing. And to be sure some of them
old wooden whalers might easy have been as old as
the Ark itself. There was a terrible great age on
some of them. . . .

" I've seen some quare sights up there, but the
quarest I can remember was the find we once made

in a liddle place—a liddle bay it was, but its name I
never heard, if it had one—that we put into one
night when the weather was rough and we up that
way for a cargo of oil. I was not in this ship then,
of course. The ship we had that time was an old
wooden schooner that's gone her ways this many a
year.

" This place I'm speakin' of must have been a
trading station or an Indian village at some time,
for there was a liddle old wharf all green and rotten,
an' ate away with them teredo beetles, the way
they get on this coast if they're built of anything
only Australian hardwood. But there wasn't a
livin' soul to be seen.

" Well, of course, we went ashore, some of us, an'
just by chance—we were pokin' about the wharf
for some loose wood to make a fire—we found a very
quare thing.

" Bones—lashin's o' bones—whole anatomies of
them, all wrapped in matting, two an' two, face to
face, an' packed away nice an' comfortable in the
piles at the back o' the wharf. Bones in themselves
don't amount to very much, for them Fish Indians
has some mighty quare ways o' buryin' themselves.
But in among these was the bones of a woman. A
wonderful tall woman she must have been. And
the great beautiful long hair of her ! As long as
your arm it was, and yellow, red yellow, like
red gold, the way I've seen it away up in the

Cariboo an' they washin' it out o' the sand of the rivers.

" An' that wasn't all, for, along with the bones o' the woman, an' the hair, there was the bones of an animal. Great large bones they was, and none of us ever saw the like of them not even the Old Man, and he was born an' rared on the coast, and knew everything that goes on legs between 'Frisco Bay and Alaska.

" We didn't make a long stay there, and I wasn't sorry, for there was a quare uncomfortable sort o' feel about it. But old Chips—he was one o' that kind that can't see anything but he must have it, if it isn't too hot or too heavy—wouldn't be content without he brought away a great long piece of the lovely gold hair and some of the bones, just to be showin' any person that wouldn't believe the yarn about them.

" But he never got them home with him, after all. We had weather that trip the like of which I never saw before or since, and I've rounded Cape Stiff many a time in my day. And at long last some of the men got talkin' among themselves about this hair an' the bones Chips had brought away with him.

" Well, it went on for a while, until one day we shipped a terrible big sea that nearly took half the watch to glory. And a fellow we had on board called Balto—a Russian Finn, he was, an' a

terrible suspicious fellow—he lets a big yell, an'
says he :

" ' The things—the things—they'll drown us
all ! '

" And with that he picks himself out o' the
scuppers and goes shamblin' into the roundhouse.
Out he comes in a second with the bits o' the dead
folks in his hand—and, whoosh ! away they goes
into a big wave, an' there was just one gleam an'
no more of the lovely gold hair trailin' away in the
foam ! "

He paused.

" And was that the end of it ? " I asked.

" It was so," said the watchman.

He pricked away at the whale's tooth for a
minute or two without speaking.

" I'm thinkin' that must have been a wonderful
fine woman," he said, " with her gold hair rollin'
down to her feet. . . ."

.   .   .   .   .

The worst of what are journalistically called
" real life stories " is that they are so seldom really
complete. They often have beginnings ; less often,
they have ends, and sometimes they have mere
middles. But they never—or hardly ever—round
themselves neatly off like story-books' happenings—
turning up all the gear, so to speak, and putting a
mousing on the cliphooks. Which, perhaps, after

all is the charm of them. It's generally the end of a story that spoils it.

I once had the beginning of a first-class adventure. I say the beginning, because, as will be seen, nothing really happened. But all the essential material was there. The people, the setting, the whole atmosphere of the thing might have been a fragment of some unfinished " Ebb Tide " or " Wreckers." It set one spinning romance on the instant.

We were fishing from the Outer Wharf at Victoria one fine, magical evening, the stars just beginning to glow in the sunset-flushed sky, a gleam of phosphorescence showing in the shadow of the piles or flashing from a line as it was drawn up from the water. A light, but rather cold, wind was blowing off the snowy summits of the Olympic Mountains across the strait, which was perhaps the reason why the black bass were sulky, and showed not the slightest interest in the fascination of the orthodox scrap of white rag flaunted before their languid noses.

There were no deep-sea ships at the wharf. A China liner had been and gone, and left some piles of interesting-looking bales and bundles ; but otherwise there was nothing but a very small coaster, rocking up and down on the tide at the inner berth, her moorings creaking on the bollards as she lifted and fell. She was so small and dark that at first you hardly noticed her ; there was no

light about her but the glimmer of the lantern a
man had just hoisted in the rigging, and a round
yellow eye that showed a cabin window. She was
a short, squat, barge-like little vessel, with one
stumpy mast, and a funnel like a stove-pipe sticking
up amidships. Her one boat gleamed white in the
half light. You could see her name—" Golconda "
—across her stern, as if she were some stately East
Indiaman at the very least, instead of a mere grubby,
uninteresting little coaster such as hang about in
shoals in the wake of the deep-sea traders on the
Pacific coast.

There did not seem to be anyone stirring about
her ; but presently a man detached himself from
her shadow and came and stood silent beside me.
I went on fishing for a while before he spoke.

" You vill not cass any more fishes to-night.
See ? "

" Probably not," I said; " not much luck this
evening."

" You vill not haf any luck while I watch you,"
he said, with a grudging laugh. " I vas very
unlucky man. See ? All my life I vas very
unlucky man ! "

This promised to be more interesting than the
coy black bass. I left off fishing and talked to the
son of ill-luck.

He proved to be the skipper of the queer little
" Golconda," a Norwegian by birth who had sailed

in Liverpool ships ever since he " vas liddle tiny
boy." His life had been chiefly in sailing ships,
and he spoke regretfully of their comfort and
cleanliness. " None of dis dirt and schmuts and
stinks "—he waved his hand in the direction of the
" Golconda," rocking peacefully at her berth.

It seemed that her business was a rather specially
odoriferous one, that of fetching and carrying
cargoes of whale oil and whale fertilizer from the
trying stations on the West Coast of Vancouver
Island. I have never had the pleasure of being to
leeward of a trying station in full blast, but I am
assured on good authority that the reducing of
leviathan to merchantable elements is one of the
most knock-down processes in the smelly line that
the human senses can meet with.

Nevertheless, whaling is one of the most ancient
and romantic of deep-sea trades, and the " Golconda's " skipper having been through the whole
business himself, could spin some interesting yarns
in his queer broken English. So we sat there on
the edge of the Outer Wharf while the afterglow
faded out of the sky, and talked—or rather he
talked—about the bowhead and the killer and the
sperm whale, about the deeds of boat steerers and
harpooners and whalers' crews, all in the brave
days gone by. For with the incoming of steam
much of the old-time glamour has gone from the
" spouter's " trade. The whalemen of the old

school say that it is owing to the advent of the
steam vessels that whales are becoming scarcer in
the Pacific, as they undoubtedly are. According
to their theory, the steamships cause such alarm
among the whales that they are keeping more and
more to the northern seas, close to the Polar ice-cap
and the Arctic Circle. However that may be, it
is certain that whales are not taken so readily as
they used to be, nor is the fishery the rousing affair
it was in the days of Herman Melville's " Moby
Dick."

It had got a trifle cold as we sat talking, and an
invitation to go on board the " Golconda " and
drink a cup of tea was far from unwelcome.

" I 'ave new Chink cook," said the skipper ;
" mein old cook he vas run avays, der galoot, an'
he take all der cake an' biscuits mit him. Der vas
noding but bread an' butter."

It was very dark on board the " Golconda," and
we groped our way along her cramped deck and so
by a black companion-way, like a scuttle leading into
hell's forecastle, into the tiny cuddy, where an
evil-looking Chinaman was shuffling in and out on
slippered feet, setting out enamel cups and saucers
on an oilcloth-covered table.

It was not until you got into the cuddy that the
" Golconda's " really salient point forced itself
upon your notice—her " aura," so to speak, the
thing of which her name would in future always

remind you. And that thing, that aura, was the smell of blubber.

It was everywhere. It was on the " Golconda " herself, without and within ; on the deck, the boat, the ropes, the rails ; in the companion and in the cabin ; on the skipper and the cook. I have not a doubt but it was also on the enamel cups and saucers, and I am quite certain it would have been in the tea. That point, however, as will be presently seen, I never put positively to the proof. It lurked, also, about one's own clothes long after-wards, and came back to you in vague, stealthy whiffs from the creases of your pocket-handkerchief.

The skipper had suddenly become quite silent. He sat down by the table, with his elbows upon it, and gnawed moodily at his nails. In the light of the smoky oil lamp I saw him for the first time—a swarthy, saturnine-looking fellow, of a dark Celtic rather than the usual fair Scandinavian type. Between the side of the vessel and the piles of the wharf the tide muttered and chuckled to itself like people talking, and somewhere in the heart of the little ship an engine kept chug-chugging.

It was perhaps out of this half-silence and the strange surroundings in the yellow, smoky light of the lamp that there grew up a queer feeling of something that was going to happen, something for which the " Golconda " was waiting, for which the silent man, nibbling his nails, was waiting, and the pulsing engine and the plotting, whispering tide. The commonplace little steamer had somehow become secret, sinister, threatening. I could no more have drunk that cup of tea than a potion brewed by a Borgia—and that not by reason of its blubbery potentialities.

Presently a large man in dungarees came on, reeking of blubber like the rest, whom the skipper introduced as " my chief mate." I don't know where the rest of the mates were, but I imagine it must have been a sort of courtesy title as regarded the " chief," as also in the case of the " chief " engineer, who came clattering down the companion, amazingly smart in his shoregoing clothes. The mate, after having fired off the surprising information that he was a " kind of cosmopolitan," became as silent as the captain. The engineer saved the situation. He talked for both in an engaging South Irish brogue, and on an amazing variety of themes. But the sense of queer, brooding expectancy remained in spite of him.

And then. . . . It may have been the smell of blubber ; it may have been the motion of the little ship as she rose and fell ; it may have been— for my part I believe it was—a sort of panic.

" Oh, dear . . . I must go ! " exclaimed my fellow-guest suddenly, and made a dash for the companion.

She said—rather lamely, in my private opinion—

that she felt queer. Everybody was very sorry. The skipper presented us with two pieces of gill bone " for curios." And the spell was broken. The " Golconda " was a commonplace little tub that smelt of blubber. And the adventure, if there was going to be one, never came off.

I wonder though. . . . A few months afterwards, a paragraph caught my eye in a local newspaper to the effect that the whaling tender " Golconda " had been burned to the water's edge on the Fraser River at Vancouver, with her crew sleeping in their bunks. My friend the cosmopolitan mate was badly burned in an attempt at rescue. As for the skipper—I don't know what became of him, but the loss of his vessel would no doubt confirm his belief that he " vas very unlucky man."

And something *had* happened after all. . . .

CHAPTER VII

A BIT OF OLD LIMEHOUSE

TIME was when Narrow Street, Limehouse, was narrow in more than name. It is something in the nature of a paradox, by the way, that in those days it was not called Narrow Street, but Fore Street, and that it only received its present name when it was widened.

Then it was little more than an alley winding between the warehouses, sail-lofts, rigging lofts, and barge-builders' sheds which lined the waterside, and the old ropewalks, long vanished, whose memory is still preserved in the name of Ropemakers' Fields. It was a region of pleasant tarry smells, where the drub of the caulkers' mallets kept up their monotonous refrain from dry dock and shipyard, and the graceful jibbooms of ships projected over the roadway as if they meant to thrust themselves through the small-paned windows of the old houses opposite.

79

Ropemakers' Fields are there still, and they sell rope and twine and suchlike details in an old shop where they sold them generations ago when Narrow Street was Fore Street. And on the other side of the way may be seen a group of old buildings which go back to the days when mast and spar made a forest along Thames-side.

In the early days of last century those buildings were, in part at any rate, a dwelling-house; for those were times when people who owned wharves and dry docks and shipyards were as proud to live at them as they were content to live by them. And there, a century and a quarter ago, was born Duncan Dunbar, one of the wealthiest of London's shipping magnates during the great era of sail.

His father was a Scotsman who had come to London and started a shipping business in a small way some time in the seventeen-eighties. He already owned the wharf in Limehouse, which has borne from that day to this the name of Dunbar Wharf, and it was there, most likely in one of the rooms which is now used as an office, that Duncan Dunbar was born.

His lot was cast in days which were good ones for shipowners. The expiration of the East India Company's monopoly had thrown open wide fields to private enterprise, and a little later the rush of emigrants to the goldfields of Australia was to give yet another fillip to passenger traffic.

Duncan Dunbar did not miss his opportunities. At his death he left a fortune of a million and a half, and his fleet was one of the finest and largest of his time. His photograph shows him as a big, stout man, the characteristic successful business type, decorated with the usual Victorian " sideboards." He was, I believe, an old bachelor, like others of his contemporaries in the shipping world. At any rate, he left no one to carry on his business, and it died with him.

When he became a wealthy man he built himself a handsome house in the East India Dock Road, and called it " Howrah House," after his dockyard at Moulmein, where so many of his ships were built. The house is still to be seen with the name conspicuously painted upon it. It is now a convent school, and probably very few of those who see it every day even wonder how it got so queer a name

The present Dunbar Wharf occupies one side of a narrow creek, which is known locally as Limekiln Creek, and a small building, which is still to be seen between the buildings which front on Narrow Street and the waterside, may be [identified—or one very like it—on an old view of Thames-side in Tudor times. This building was formerly a limekiln, and the " smoke of its burning" is plainly to be seen going up in the old picture. From this and other " lime oasts " or " limehouses " came no doubt the name of the district, and not from the

6

very problematical " lime hursts," or groves of lime trees, from which some have sought to derive it.

In Duncan Dunbar's time the wharf extended along both sides of the creek, including that part which is now occupied by the Dundee Steam Navigation Company. Here were to be found his sail-lofts, rigging lofts, warehouses, and storehouses ; in short, all the shore establishment of a big sailing fleet. Duncan Dunbar never built ships on Thames-side like the Wigrams and the Greens, though he had (as already mentioned) a shipyard of his own at Moulmein. Like John Willis, he swore by teak. There are pieces of teak doing good service about the wharf to-day as parts of ladders and doors, which have no doubt travelled the world a good deal in their time when they formed part of one or other of the Dunbar fleet.

These " country-built " East Indiamen were amazingly durable. The British Blackwallers only carried a fourteen years' class, with an extension subject to further survey, and some of them became extremely leaky towards the end of their career. A writer in the " Nautical Magazine " during the 'sixties makes some very strong comments on the state of certain of the ships engaged in carrying emigrants during the boom. But the teak-built vessels from the Indian and Burmese yards were wonderfully long-lived. Lieutenant Coates testified from personal observation to the soundness of the

DUNBAR WHARF

old " Java's " timbers when she was eighty years of age, although, of course, a ship which might be perfectly tight when lying quietly in harbour might be a very different tale when working and straining in a seaway. The " Edwin Fox," the old " Coldstream," and the " Lincelles " are other examples ; in fact, most of the specimens of longevity among foreign-going wooden ships will be found to have been country built. And it is hardly to be wondered at. These ships were built throughout of three layers of solid teak ; and teak resists, as no other wood is able to, the effects of weather conditions in the Tropics.

And when a teak-built vessel was at the end of her tether she would always fetch a good price if she could manage to hobble over to the Mauritius, to be cut up for making shingles.

One of the interesting relics at the wharf is the cabin table—teak again—of the old " Hougomont," one of the Moulmein ships built in 1852. There is a very fine model of this ship in the Trinity House. She was one of the best-known of the ships which used to carry cargoes of the Englishman's national beverage out to hearten him in his exile. (Hence the familiar term " India Pale Ale ! ") And in the old rigging lofts where one may look out and see a barge or a west country ketch lying beside the wharf, and get a glimpse of the busy shipping beyond, the floors are still thick with the deposits of tar which have been there since they set up the rigging for the Dunbar ships which were engaged as transports in the days of the Crimean War.

. . . . .

Most of the Dunbar ships were named after British victories ashore and afloat, and more than one name was duplicated in the fleet of some other firm, as well as in the " Navy List." Indeed, it must be confessed that—unless they did it on purpose !—the various Thames-side owners showed remarkably little resource in the matter of christening their ships.

Thus there was an " Agincourt," a " Trafalgar," and a " Nile " in both Dunbar's and Green's fleet. Dunbar's " Blenheim," built in 1845, was followed by Smith's much larger and more renowned ship of the same name. Wigram and Marshall had each an " Essex." And there have been " La Hogues," " Camperdowns," " Ramillies," and " Aboukirs " in the Navy ever since those battles were fought.

A friend of mine had an old shipmate who started his sea career in Dunbar's " Talavera." Her skipper, he used to say, had his royals made of Number One canvas, and hung on to them until they blew out of the bolt ropes, which seems to suggest that cracking on was not unknown even among the sedate Blackwallers.

The biggest vessel Duncan Dunbar ever owned was named after himself. She was a ship of nearly fourteen hundred tons, built by Laing of Sunderland in 1855. Her loss, by stranding on the Rocas reef when outward bound in 1865, caused considerable discussion. Nobody was officially blamed for the disaster, but a good many pretty severe strictures were passed at the time by writers in the nautical papers. " The ' Duncan Dunbar ' was groping her way in the dark, and the blue pigeon was not flying," was one comment.

However, no lives were lost, though the passengers spent a rather uncomfortable few days on the sandspit before they were taken off by the Royal Mail Steamer " Oneida."

The " Dunbar " was lost just outside Sydney Harbour with only one survivor, a seaman named Johnstone, on the night of August 20, 1857. How it happened will never really be known. But the most likely explanation seems that the captain was trying to wear ship to give himself more sea room and was driven on the lee shore while doing so, thinking himself, no doubt, a little further from the rocks than was actually the case.

One of the best-known ships in the fleet was the old " La Hogue," also built at Laing's yard in 1858, which came under Messrs. Devitt & Moore's flag after Duncan Dunbar's death. She was a very popular ship in the Australian passenger trade, and made some very fine runs with wool, in which she beat many of the crack iron clippers.

Duncan Dunbar only had one ship in the China tea trade, and that was the " Northfleet," famed in connexion with one of the saddest of the sea disasters of last century.

She was built at Northfleet, on the Thames, and while she was in the tea trade she made some very speedy passages, although she was in no sense a clipper in appearance. In the 'seventies she was put into the emigrant trade, and in January, 1875, left London with over three hundred navvies on board, bound for Tasmania. Her commander, Captain Knowles, had just been appointed to her, and his wife was to accompany him on his first voyage.

Bad weather delayed the ship at the start, and she anchored for the night off Dungeness. The night was dark, but not foggy, the usual look-out was posted, and the lights were burning brightly. Most of the emigrants had gone below, when a steamer bore straight down on the " Northfleet " and struck her amidships.

The rest of the story may be pieced together from the narratives of the survivors.

" The pilot passed the word," said one man, a seaman, " to drop anchor off Dungeness. Here we lay snug enough, and at eight o'clock the watch was set, Frank Sealove and John Gunstaveson being on

deck and on the watch ; they died doing their
duty. I went down to my berth, and was soon
fast asleep. I don't know how long I had slept,
when I was nearly shaken out of my hammock "
(the Blackwallers' crews were provided with hammocks instead of the berths usual in merchant
ships) " by a fearful crashing and a staggering over
of the ship, as if she had been struck by a broadside
of cannon shot. Before I knew where I was, being
awoke so suddenly, I heard the boatswain sing out,
' All hands on deck to the pumps.' I was not long
in jumping into my boots, I can tell you, and all
in the forecastle ran on deck pell-mell. When we
got there we could not see much, for the night was
dark, but there was light enough to see a half-
dressed crowd come rushing madly up from the
steerage passenger berths, and you didn't want any
light to hear the shrieks of the women and the
crying of the children. Most of the men went to
the pumps, which had forty pairs of willing hands
working at them for dear life. I went down below
with the carpenter to examine the leak, and we soon
found that we might as well try to pump the
Channel dry as keep the ship clear of water ; in fact,
trying to pump the Channel dry was just what we
were doing, for there was a hole stove in the ship's
quarter which was quickly leaving not a line to
choose between the English Channel and the hold
of the ' Northfleet.' The carpenter tried to stuff a

great piece of tow into the hole, but it just went quietly through, as if you were shoving a rope's end through a porthole."

In the meantime the unknown steamer which had run the " Northfleet " down had sheered off without attempting to render any assistance.

" When we got on deck " (says another survivor's narrative, this time a passenger) " it was dark, and yet not so dark but that we could see about us. There was one light at the masthead, the two others, the red and the green, being away under the bow. Just as we got up there was another crash, and we heard the mate, who was a north-countryman, shouting to somebody, though we could not at the moment see either him or them. As we came running towards him we saw a big vessel right against us, with her bow so near that I could have jumped on to her, and a lot of men running about on her jabbering in a tongue that we could not understand. Then the mate turned to me and said, ' I can't understand what they say. You run down below and tell that French fellow to come up ; perhaps he can talk to them '—for we had a French fellow amongst us.

" As I was turning round to go down I saw the foreigner bearing round with her stern to ours, and a lot of the crew running to the bow with a piece of tarpaulin, which they threw over the figurehead so as to hide her name. With that she backed water and got clear of us. The mate was shouting to them all the time, and when he saw this he cried out, ' Oh, my God ! stop and save us, for we have four hundred emigrants on board ! ' but it was not a bit of use, for she backed water and shot ahead across our bow, and was away with her black smoke blowing in our faces before we could say many words to each other."

The " Northfleet " disaster was one of those in which every possible circumstance seems to combine to bring about unnecessary loss of life. The captain was desperately sending up blue lights from the poop, but, although there were many ships anchored close by, not one of them took any heed. Probably they had no idea that the signals were signals of distress. Ships in those waters were constantly sending up signals for a pilot, and it was no doubt thought that these were something of the kind. One ship, an Australian clipper, was lying so close to the " Northfleet " that she could not have helped hearing the cries for help, but as luck would have it her look-out man was a Dutchman, and either so stupid or so indifferent that he did not think it worth while to rouse out the watch. The signal gun failed to fire.

Attempts were now being made to lower the boats. Probably the reason this was not done at once was because help from the ships close at hand had been so confidently looked for that it was thought there would be more danger to life in lowering the boats than in waiting to be taken off by another vessel.

The emigrants—and in particular the navvies—had until now been in a state of stupor. This now began to give place to panic, and they began to try to rush the boats as they were lowered by sliding down the falls.

" There was a terrible panic," says the survivor's tale, " amongst the strong, rough men when it became apparent that the vessel was sinking. The wild rush for the boats and the mad confusion that took place was like the trampling of a herd of buffaloes. Poor Captain Knowles, brave as a hero all the time, was nevertheless angered at the reckless selfishness of the men, and he drew a pistol and threatened the big fellows who were leaping helter-skelter into the boats. He said, ' The boats are for women and children, not for such as you.'

" One man was shot in the thigh while trying to get into a boat, but he fell into the boat and was one of those who was saved. Mrs. Knowles sat quietly by the boatswain in the bow, and, when the boat was pushed off, her husband waved his hands to her, saying, ' Good-bye, my dear, good-bye ! '

" ' Good-bye, my love,' she called back.

" ' Take care of my wife, bos'n,' cried the captain.

" ' I will, captain,' answered the boatswain, ' if she goes I will go too.' "

A few seconds later—twenty minutes more or less after the first shock—the " Northfleet " plunged and sank bows first.

The identity of the foreign steamer whose captain had behaved so callously towards the victims of his reckless navigation was never definitely established. The Spanish ship " Murillo " was detained in Cadiz under suspicion for some months; it was proved that she had been in collision in the vicinity of Dungeness on the night in question and at the time the " Northfleet " was struck, but the captain stoutly denied that any damage had been done. He got off scot free, but he must have felt the brand of Cain upon him for the rest of his days.

.   .   .   .   .

The " Cospatrick " was built at Moulmein in 1856. She was an Indiaman of the real old type, with painted ports and stern and quarter galleries. In 1863 she took out the submarine cable to the Persian Gulf, and laid the last two or three hundred miles of it from near Jack to Kurrachee. On the return journey she brought troops home from India, and for her next two voyages was engaged in trooping out and home. Her commander at that time was Captain James Elmslie, who had served in the " La Hogue " and the " Parramatta," and was later to become one of the best-known officers on the Australian run as captain of the famous " Sobraon."

A letter from one of her midshipmen, dated March 29, 1864, " in a dead calm off the island of Socotra," gives some interesting particulars of the cable-laying episode.

" We are now becalmed," the letter begins, " off the N.E. point of the island of Socotra, and I am just sent below because my hands (at least the backs of them) and my face are all covered with spots and very much swollen ; it is what they call the prickly heat. I have written two or three letters already, but I shall not send them, as I will tell you all the news up to the present in this. . . . I will just give you all the news about the passage here, beginning when we left. We left Gravesend on a Friday ; on Saturday we passed Brighton (we saw Deal and Dover also, but could not make out Eastbourne), and at 12 p.m. Saturday night the pilot left us, taking ashore letters, one of which I hope you received. As I was writing it I felt rather sea-sick, and it soon proved to be the case. I ate nothing for three days, as I could get nothing but salt junk and biscuit, neither of which I could eat ; but on Wednesday the steward thought I might possibly like something, so he sent me in some soup, which I quickly demolished, and in the evening I got some milk, so I felt pretty well all right. But I forgot to tell you on Monday it came on to blow rather fresh, and increased, till on Tuesday we had quite a gale, hove-to under close-reefed fore and main topsails. They were up nearly all night taking in the sails, pouring rain and something like wind. I was sent below because I was no good, being as weak as a child from sea-sickness. In our house all the chests were floating about, and there was real confusion, but we got over it all right, excepting that we stove in one side of one of our boats and lost 900 gallons of water, which we are now feeling the want of. We are come to this island to see if we can't get some when we can get a little nearer. One day soon after in the Bay of Biscay the engineer (you saw the little engine, or bulgine, as we call it : it is to pump the tanks with the cable in full) was nowhere to be found, so the Captain said he should put in to Madeira for another, as we thought the poor fellow had fallen overboard and been drowned and we had not heard him. We all believed he was drowned, so we had got all our letters ready to send home when the carpenter saw what he at first took to be the engineer's ghost, but which soon turned out to be the engineer himself standing at the door of their berth. It seems he had fallen down in a fit while in the hold looking after the tanks (where they had looked but had not seen anything of him) and had just recovered ; so " (is the writer's naïve comment) " we had our first disappointment.

" Nothing particular happened till Christmas Day, when we did no work and had a bottle of beer each. About three weeks after we left, the captain told Sails (the sailmaker) to make hammocks for two of is, and so Wardroper and Foster had them and have not slept in the berth since.

" At twelve p.m. on the last day of 1863 we all got together with tin pots and one concertina and made a fearful row, marching round the decks until the captain and all the passengers had turned out. They gave us all some grog to let them go to sleep again, which we did after half an hour more at it.

" On the 2nd of January we crossed the Line, when at 12.30 p.m. we saw Neptune (I forgot to tell you he paid us a visit the night before and we sent him afloat again) in his car drawn by four men, dressed up to represent seadogs, on their hands and knees. He came along the decks, with the barber and the whole lot of them, and we (those that had not crossed the Line before, being all the passengers, three of us, and two sailors who had been in the Hudson's Bay and Mediterranean service) were all duly brought up on to the platform, shaved with rusty pieces of iron with notches in them, and then very gently (as you may imagine) precipitated backward into a sail full of water, where the seadogs caught you and ducked you till the next one came.

" Then nothing particular occurred till we saw a little rocky island with no inhabitants, called Trinidad (not the Trinidad in the West Indies), only a few miles square. This was the first land we saw since we lost sight of our native shores."

This island of Trinidad is a place as wild and desolate as the mind of man could conceive, and it has associations as strange and romantic as any spot in the Seven Seas.

Lonely, barren, forbidding, it rises sheer out of the South Atlantic some hundreds of miles from the coast of Brazil. The seas breaking upon it send sheets of foam two hundred feet into the air, and its riven volcanic peaks are perpetually wreathed in shifting cloud shapes. Bygone convulsions of nature have destroyed the forest which it is thought once clad its sides, and only a thin covering of red earth hides the naked rock. Its iron-bound shores are strewn with the wreckage of centuries, and haunted by swarms of nightmare-like land crabs which have even been known to attack human beings.

But this bleak spot has been for the past hundred years a lodestone to the adventurous. For it is one of the few really authentic " treasure islands," the precise hoard said to have been cached upon it being the church plate carried away from Lima Cathedral during the South American Wars of Liberation in 1820.

In the early years of the nineteenth century, be it remembered, the pirate was no mere legendary being, as he is to-day. He was a real factor to reckon with. There was at that time precious little romance about him. His calling, like that of the "high toby man," was sadly degraded. Men like the early buccaneers were men born a generation too late. They held to the tradition of Drake and his school, and they had the misfortune to live in an age which no longer considered it a virtuous act to sack a Spanish city or plunder a Plate fleet. It was a narrow line which separated such men from the privateer.

But those days were gone. Gone the days of Morgan, of Davis, of Sawkins, of Bartholomew Sharpe, of Dampier. Gone the old-style buccaneers with whom Prince Rupert thought it no shame to cruise and carouse. And in their stead had arisen a school of cowardly cut-throats, murderers, gallows-birds—the sweepings of seaports, the off-scourings of the forecastles of all the nations.

All the wealth of Lima was hastily put on board any vessels which were available, and it is hardly wonderful that a considerable proportion of it never reached its rightful destination. No doubt in some cases the crews of the ships themselves took possession of ship and treasure ; and to the hungry sea jackals who lurked about the path of shipping in the South Pacific and Atlantic Oceans others fell an easy prey.

One of these pirates it was who captured the ship

carrying the cathedral plate, and afterwards, so the tale goes, hid it on the island of Trinidad—and hid it so well that no one has ever been able to set eyes on it since. One story says that it was the notorious Benito de Soto, a Portuguese whose rakish black brigantine, the "Black Joke," was at one time the terror of peaceful merchantmen in the South Atlantic. But the dates do not tally. The Lima treasure was on the water in 1820 or 1821, and Benito de Soto's piratical career did not begin until 1827.

The fact is, however, established that a gang of pirates were executed in Havana for having been concerned in plundering ships carrying treasure from Lima; and about 1850 a man who professed to be the sole survivor of the gang revealed on his death-bed the secret of the hoard. This man had been a quartermaster in a British opium clipper, where he had always been known as " the Pirate " on account of his sinister appearance and his mysterious past. The captain had shown him kindness, and by way of showing his gratitude the pirate, knowing himself to be dying, gave him a rough chart drawn on canvas of the island of Trinidad, where, he went on to say, a great quantity of treasure taken from the cathedral of Lima lay buried at the foot of the mountain called on the map " the Sugar Loaf."

The yarn came to the ears of Mr. E. F. Knight, afterwards to become famous as a war correspondent

7

in the Boer War and elsewhere, and he was so much impressed by its plausibility that he fitted out his yacht " Alerte " and sailed for the island. After three months' strenuous work the quest was abandoned ; but Mr. Knight still believed implicitly in the truth of the story.

There are undeniably one or two weak points in it. One would hardly have thought that the pirates would have chosen a place presenting such serious difficulties in the landing of their booty, or in the removal of it when the time came.

But the chief flaw is the fact that no treasure has been found, nor any trace of treasure. What has become of it ? Had it, as a matter of fact, been found and removed by one of the earlier expeditions, and had the finders decided to say nothing about it, in case of the Crown stepping in and claiming it as treasure trove, the island having been formally annexed so long ago as 1700 ? It is by no means unlikely, especially in view of the fact that both those who first visited the place seem to have abandoned the search in an astonishingly short time. One would hardly think that it would have been buried deep—unless, indeed, some volcanic disturbance, such as that which originally formed the island from the depths of the sea, has so effectively swallowed up the booty as to put it out of the reach of treasure seekers until the day of doom.

"Then (continues the letter) we had another gale of wind, only not quite so bad as that in the Channel. Soon after we sighted a ship and found she was the 'Henry Moore,' and the next day, as we were within half a mile and it was a dead calm, the skipper came aboard and ours returned the compliment. The day after we had a fair wind and left her astern. We had a storm rounding the Cape, but instead of being cold, as I expected, it was as warm as it is on Midsummer day in England all the way (we went several degrees south of it), and in fact ever since about a fortnight after we left it has been as warm, and generally warmer, except in the storms we have had. The wind blew continually from the east, so we were obliged to go up the Mozambique Channel instead of going the usual track round by the Mauritius, where we had plenty of work: every four hours tacking, keeping a continual look-out at the masthead, and the thermometer up to 120; they think it would have risen higher only the instrument didn't go any higher.

"Well, after we had had a good spell of this weather, about three weeks, and no wind all the time, all at once we had a change, awful heavy rain and wind, the same for three or four days. Every time we went below we put on a dry suit, and when we went on deck again for our next watch we changed back so as to keep dry and comfortable in our watch below. Then when we got all clear of that the captain said he should put in at Johanna to get water. It is a town in an island of the same name at the top of the channel. So we went on working away as before till we sighted land for the second time since we left. We could not tell what it was until we got quite close, when we found it was another island called Mayotta. Soon after we arrived off the island a boat came off with an Arab pilot, who wanted to pilot us in, and half a dozen natives, all Arabs. The pilot could speak French, and as we have a good many who can speak it, as well as two French people, we got on all right. He said he was sent by the French governor, and told us all about Johanna, and the winds and currents, etc. Soon after a fine breeze sprang up, so we stood off : another disappointment, as we were all promised to go ashore.

" Since that nothing has happened till we arrived here, except that we sighted the Zanzibar coast for a day or two. But I must not forget to tell you that we had fresh pork one day, when we killed the big pig, and it happened to be Wraugham's birthday, the 23rd of February. It may seem very funny of me to tell you this, but it is quite like an anniversary.

" March 30th.—Chief officer went ashore with six hands each with a cutlass and gun. They saw lots of natives, who all ran away, and flocks of goats, one of which they shot. In the afternoon a fishing boat came alongside and gave us lots of fish for three rupees and a bucketful of biscuit.

"March 31st.—Boat went ashore again in fore-noon and native boat came alongside. We took a whole lot of water melons and pumpkins and dates and a bucketful of all different kinds of pretty little fish, and gave them two rupees and a bucketful of biscuit and sent them away. In the afternoon had a fair wind, so went right round the point and into a sort of harbour and dropped anchor. At 8 p.m. our boat came alongside with a pretty little brown kid (alive) and some fruit.

"April 1st.—The captain went ashore early and found a convenient pond not far from the shore near the town. . . . None of the houses have roofs —they are simply high brick walls with some white stuff over them, from six to a dozen yards square, with one big hole for a door and two or three little ones for windows; but the Sultan's palace, as they call it, is a round building with a roof something like some of those queer concerns at the Pavilion at Brighton. There are not more than thirty houses or so built here and there round the Sultan's palace, and there are a great many gardens quite separate from the houses and fenced round."

.   .   .   .   .

Early in the 'seventies the "Cospatrick" was purchased by Messrs. Shaw, Savill & Co. for £10,000

for the New Zealand emigrant trade. She left
Gravesend on September 11, 1874. It was her
second voyage under her new house flag, and it was
to be her last.

She had on board 429 emigrants, men, women,
and children, bound for Auckland. Her commander
Captain Elmslie, was a brother of her previous
captain, with whom he had sailed as chief officer,
succeeding to the command of the " Cospatrick "
when his brother went to the " Sobraon."

The usual stories were of course told after the
event about people having refused at the last
moment to sail in the ship owing to premonitions
that she was destined to meet with misfortune.
Such yarns nearly always get about after a great
sea disaster. And as a matter of fact the " Cospatrick " was a perfectly sound and seaworthy ship,
although she was nearly twenty years old. She
was a Moulmein-built teak vessel, than which there
could be none more durable, and she was classed
A1 at Lloyd's until 1883. There are, indeed,
always a certain number of passengers in any list
who do not actually sail in the ship for one reason
or another, and if she gets to her destination safely
no one hears of their " premonitions."

Everything went well until the night of November
17th, when the ship was in lat. 37 S. and long. 12 E.
The second officer went below, leaving all well,
only to be roused out half an hour later by the

dreaded cry of " Fire ! " It was soon evident that
the ship was doomed. The boats in the forepart
of the ship were involved in the flames, and of those
which remained only two got clear of the ship.
Eighty of the terrified emigrants crowded into one
of the quarter-boats, and remained in it until the
davits gave way and it fell into the water stern
first, drowning all those in it.

The masts crashed over the side one by one,
killing many of those on board in their fall, and
finally the whole of the ship's stern was blown out,
probably by the gases which had been generated
by the fire, for there were no explosives on board.
The captain had remained on the poop till the end,
his wife, who had refused to leave him, by his side.
When the last moment came he first took her in
his arms and threw her overboard, then leapt after
her into the sea, and at the same time the ship's
doctor, who had elected to share their fate, jumped
overboard with the captain's child in his arms.

They were more fortunate than the people in
the two boats. In one of these, commanded by the
chief officer, were thirty-two persons, of whom
twenty-five were passengers. In the second, with
the second officer, Henry Macdonald, were thirty-
nine. The boats kept together for a couple of days,
when they lost sight of each other in a storm, and
the chief officer's boat was never heard of again.
Those in the remaining boat suffered terribly from

hunger and thirst. They were without food or water, mast or sail. One by one they perished raving mad through drinking sea water, and finally only five were left, these having been driven in their extremity to eating the dead bodies of their companions in misfortune.

On the 27th a ship was sighted, and although she passed without seeing the signals from the boat, owing to the high seas which were running at the time, the wretched survivors took hope. They realized that they were in the track of shipping, and had a chance of being picked up. And it was not long before another vessel, the " British Sceptre," sighted the boat and took them on board. Only three lived to tell the tale, and one of these, Edward Cotter, is still living, and not long since recounted the story of his escape to a representative of a London newspaper.

The cause of the disaster was of course never known, though it has since been stated that all the lamps which were carried were not properly equipped with safety appliances.

CHAPTER VIII

FIGUREHEADS

Mysterious Disappearance of a Gentleman—A Figurehead's Long Voyage—A New Sort of Ghost—The Evolution of the Figurehead—Blindfolding the Lion—A Wonderful Sculpture Gallery.

IT is strange how a ship calls to the ship-lover —so that you feel you must give up whatever business or pleasure you happen to be intent upon at the moment and go in quest of her.

The masts and yards of a square-rigger had beckoned to me over the sheds in the East India Dock, and I descended from the top of the 'bus without more ado and answered the summons.

There had seemed a something familiar about her all along, though I cannot lay claim to that mysterious sort of sixth sense possessed by some old sailors, which enabled them to reconstruct a whole ship from a glimpse of her trucks over the top of a shed, much as savants reconstruct mammoths and ichthyosauri from two or three fossil bones, or Scotland Yard experts a crime from a cigarette ash and an unwashed tumbler. But she turned out to be an old acquaintance of mine right enough—

none other than the old " Robert Scrafton," a
Norwegian-owned and (I believe) Norwegian-built
ship which used to sport a figurehead of a gentleman in the correct garb of civilization, frock-
coat, stickup collar, and all complete. It was, I
think, a portrait of the owner, or perhaps the
builder.

Well, here she was, but—the gentleman in the
frock-coat was gone ! You could see the little holes
where he had been bolted on, but otherwise it was
as if he had never been. What had happened to
him, I wonder ? I couldn't get anything but
Scandinavian grunts out of the members of the
crew who were visible, which was unusual, since
Baltic, especially Finnish, crews usually speak
excellent English.

Perhaps he had only been unshipped for reasons
of safety, and was all the while stowed away somewhere on board. But I don't think so. I have seen
the ship in port several times, and never missed
from her bow his flowing coat-tails and benevolent
whiskers.

No ! It may well be that one of old Ocean's
daughters may have taken a fancy to him, and
induced her parent to tear him from his place and
bear him down to the caves

> Where great whales go sailing by,
> Sail and sail with unshut eye
> Round the world for ever and aye. . . .

Does he, like Lycidas, " visit the bottom of the monstrous world " ?   Or will he drift on the ocean currents until he is washed ashore on some sunlit isle of the South, where, his decorous head crowned with hibiscus, he sees *kava* ceremonially imbibed, and even, it may be, " long pig " sacrificed in his honour ?

It is amazing what long distances fruit, nuts, leaves, trees, and the wreckage of ships can be carried by the currents.   There are, I believe, cases on record of West Indian native work being washed ashore on the western islands of Scotland.   Some parts of the coast of Cornwall are strewn with tiny shells carried across the Atlantic on the Gulf Stream.   And the lion figurehead of Devitt and Moore's clipper ship " Rodney," washed away in the Bay of Biscay on November 30, 1895, came ashore six months later in Whitesand Bay.   A similar occurrence is recorded regarding the figurehead of the Australian emigrant clipper " Blue Jacket," which was washed ashore two years after the ship had been abandoned on fire.

The last time I saw that frock-coated gentleman I spoke of was in the Surrey Docks a year or two ago, when there were no less than four ships with figureheads in the same dock at one time—rather an unusual occurrence nowadays.

One of the others, if I remember rightly, was the " Endymion," now called " Virgo." Her figurehead also was a bearded gentleman, but in his case the costume was classic. He held in his hand a round object, which I suppose was intended to represent the moon, though it looked more like an orange. He wasn't really in the least one's idea of the shepherd beloved of Diana ; but the rôle of Endymion at any rate fitted him better than that of Virgo !

There was also, I believe, the " Alejandrina," whose romantic return from the dead, so to speak, created such a stir in shipping circles at the time, and a little barque, the " Braemar." Both of them had allegorical females for figureheads, in the fashion of the period immediately preceding that of the meaningless yellow (not even gilt) scroll which was the last sadly degenerate phase of the figurehead.

.   .   .   .   .

There have been cases of figureheads which wore not only frock-coats but top-hats ! One such— perhaps the best-known—was that of the celebrated clipper ship " Samuel Plimsoll " ; and indeed I believe the sailor's champion is still to be seen thus arrayed on the old ship's bow where she lies moored in Fremantle Harbour. Another example was the figurehead of the " Edwin Fox," one of Duncan Dunbar's Moulmein-built Blackwallers, which was bought by Shaw, Savill & Co. for the New Zealand trade.

Rather a good yarn is told about this ship. She had been put into dry dock at Dunkirk while search was made for a mysterious leak which had baffled everybody for a long time. The cause was eventually discovered to be a hole which had been made when the ship had a condenser on board. The condenser had been removed, and the hole had either never been stopped or else the stopping had worked out again.

A new captain and crew took her over in Dunkirk, whence she was bound for Cardiff in ballast. She had not been very long at sea before one of the hands had occasion to go down the forehatch, but he had not been gone many seconds when he came bolting up on deck again as if Old Nick were at his heels !

" Hallo," said the mate, " what's up ? *You're* in a devil of a hurry for once ! And why the blazes didn't you stop down there till you'd done what you were sent for ? "

" I ain'd goen down there no more, mister," said the man, a Swede ; " dot arn'd no good."

Well, the mate could make nothing of him, so he sent a couple of hands in his place.

Up they came the next minute in a big hurry.

" Oh, gobbressmysoul, mister mate," yelled one of them, a nigger, his face green with fright, " ef dar ain't a great big h'ant down in dat forehold ! "

" H'ant nothing ! " growled the mate. " **Too**

much Dunkirk gin, that's what's the matter. Here, bos'n, you go and have a look what these idiots are gibbering about."

The bos'n then went below; but he also reappeared rather quicker than he had gone.

" That's right, sir," he said. " I seen him all right."

" Seen what ? " barked the mate.

" Why, the bloke ! "

" Bloke ?   What bloke ?   If there's a bloke down there, he's no business there.   I'll bloke him ! "

The skipper had by this time arrived on the scene.

" Better go down yourself, Mr. Roy," he said, " and see what all this means. And if there's anyone hiding down there fetch him up."

The mate seized a handspike and dived below.

Presently he returned, looking distinctly sheepish, and without the looked-for captive.

" There—there *is* a man there, sir," he reported.

" A man ?   Well, who is he ?   Did you speak to him ? "

" I don't know, sir, not exactly."

However, Captain Johnson wasn't the sort of man to let a h'ant scare him out of his own forehold, so down he went to see for himself.

And sure enough he got a nasty start !

There, starting out of the gloom of the forehold, was a tall white figure with arm upraised as if in warning or menace.

But the skipper stood his ground valiantly, and, finding the figure didn't move, he took heart of grace and advanced.

It was the counterfeit presentment of Edwin Fox, Esquire, which had been removed while the leak was being repaired, and lashed against the foremast in such a way that it looked just like a threatening ghost in the half-light.

Well, the mate and the bos'n didn't hear the last of it from the skipper for a long time. But he had a bit of a scare himself, all the same.

. . . . .

The habit is well-nigh as old as the world of placing some kind of an image or device at the bow of a ship, usually connected in some way with the vessel's name. It dates back to the dawn of navigation, and it went on until the coming of the steamship brought about a break in the continuity of shipbuilding development.

It was the instinct of man even in the earliest ages to adorn his ship—to lavish upon her decoration and endearment, as upon a woman beautiful and beloved. And it is that same instinct—or rather combination of instincts—which makes his modern descendant perch a graceful nude statuette or a grotesque squatting " Billiken " on the bonnet of his motor-car, which he calls his mascot.

Like most such instincts, it arose from a complication of motives. There was, as we have said, the desire to make the beloved thing beautiful. There was also the practical aspect. What more natural than to finish off the rough ends of the bow timbers in the shape of some kind of a fanciful device ? In its first phase (and to a certain extent in its last) the figurehead was an integral part of the hull ; it was only in its intermediate period that it became a separate and superimposed structure, more or less ponderous and elaborate.

But there was also the desire to put both ship and owner under the protection of some powerful spiritual guardian. For, apart from the ordinary risks of war and of storms, the sea to the primitive navigator was a place of many and unknown terrors—of witches afloat in eggshells, of etins, of nicors, of dragons, of sea serpents. What more likely, when there was a special saint or a special god for nearly everything under the sun, than that there should be those whose particular business it was to look after sailor-folk ?

So the Argonauts nailed a bough of the sacred talking oak to the beak of Argo. The ancient Greek poised his exquisite Winged Victory at the prow of his fighting ship. The Viking shaped the curving bow-timbers of his longship into the semblance of serpent or dragon, called her his love, his darling, his Long Serpent, patted her sides, praised her for her swiftness, and launched her into the unknown seas with the blood of goats red on her keel. Even the fierce Coast Indian of British Columbia set up his grotesquely carved totem pole in the prow of his war canoe to serve the dual purpose of protecting himself and her and alarming his enemies by its hideousness. And the Spaniard of the sixteenth century invoked the aid of Madonna and saint, whose images looked out from the bows of their rolling galleons, laden with the gold of the Indies, or strewed the shores of Britain from Land's End to Cape Wrath, when the great Armada went to wrack.

The custom is one as universal as it is ancient. The Chinese are, I believe, the only race among whom the figurehead is unknown ; and even they paint a realistic pair of eyes in the bows of their junks, so that the vessel may be able to see where she is going, a habit which, oddly enough, also prevails among the Maltese.

And that reminds me of a yarn I once heard about a certain famous clipper ship. She was bound to Brisbane, whereas her usual port was Sydney, and as she was beating up the Australian coast against the usual southerly current and contrary winds, she got just as far as Sydney, and could get no further.

At last said the skipper to the mate in despair :

" You see that old devil for'ard there, mister ? "

8

indicating the handsome lion which pranced proudly
at the clipper's bow. " It's my belief he can *see*
Sydney, and he won't go past. Just you get a
tarpaulin and put it over his head, and we'll see if
we can get past Sydney then ! "

And sure enough the mate fetched a tarpaulin
and solemnly blindfolded the lion ! Of course the
ship did get past Sydney, or else she'd have been
there yet ; but I don't know if the tarpaulin had
anything to do with it.

   .   .   .   .   .

During the thirteenth and fourteenth centuries
the figurehead was in temporary eclipse. Ships of
that period had usually a bow platform—the
original " forecastle " whose name is still retained,
while that of the stern-castle has entirely disappeared—which projected right over the stem of
the ship, and was generally, as models and pictures
show, hung round with shields bearing heraldic
devices. In the fifteenth century the forecastle
gradually became less of a superimposed edifice and
more a part of the vessel herself, and the heraldic
adornments too began to be transferred to the beak
of the ship ; thus, in a model of a Venetian galleass
of the period the Lion of St. Mark is shown as a
figurehead.

All through the fifteenth and sixteenth centuries
ships showed a steady tendency to become more

ornate—a tendency which, however, was more evident as regarded the stern than the bow, the apple-cheeked shape of the latter and the large square spritsail rigged under the bowsprit no doubt militating against much adornment there.

It is not until the Tudor times that we find the figurehead as we know it beginning to take shape. Many of the models of ships of the period show a conventional lion finishing off the swelling curve of the stem, such as may be seen in all the existing reconstructions of the "Harry Grâce à Dieu" at Greenwich and elsewhere. It should of course be borne in mind that all the models of that famous ship are to a certain extent pure guesswork. No one knows positively what the "Great Harry"— which I saw somewhere the other day rather naïvely described as the "Old Harry"!—was like in detail. Some of the Tudor ships show a little figure perched mascot-fashion on the forecastle. Drake's "Golden Hynde" and Grenville's "Revenge" are cases in point; but since the "Golden Hynde" and (I believe) the "Revenge" also had been renamed, the figures were probably placed there at the time of the rechristening.

By the middle of the seventeenth century stern and quarter had become one mass of elaborate carving—Tritons, Nereids, dolphins, sea-horses, Caryatids, Atlantids, and the Lord knows what in the way of mythological and allegorical beings.

The art of the ship-carver had reached its greatest elaboration with Grinling Gibbons working at the Deptford Navy Yard. Decoration ran riot, and the bows of the unhandy, wallowing monsters of the period were encrusted with devices which— however beautiful as specimens of craftsmanship— were far more suited for the adornment of a mantel-piece or a four-post bed than a vessel going into action or labouring in a seaway. "One great heaving play of dolphins and a Neptune or so reining in webby-footed sea-horses, and Arion with his harp high atop of them," says Hal o' the Draft in Mr. Kipling's story " The Wrong Thing," describing the scroll-work he designed for King Henry the Seventh's ship—and the description is one which might with equal, perhaps with greater, aptness be applied to the ships of the later Stuart period. Tudor ships, as we have seen, were generally marked by a certain austerity of design, and what decoration they had was usually confined to the stern.

During the eighteenth century all this elaborate " gingerbread work " began to be gradually dispensed with. The conventional lion figurehead, too, dropped out of use, and in its place came in a great variety of subjects, Roman and Greek warriors, periwigged admirals, turbaned potentates, all executed in that somewhat pompous manner characteristic of the period, so that the figurehead of the ship of the line displayed a strong family likeness to the Georgian monuments in the Abbey. The pervading classicism of the times was reflected in the naming of ships as in literature and art, and consequently in their figureheads : so that "Orions " and " Hectors," " Neptunes " and " Ajaxes " supplanted the old English fleet names, " Prince Royal," " Sovereign of the Seas," " Lion," and " Tiger." A characteristic specimen is to be seen in the " Orion " figurehead outside the Royal United Service Institution Museum in Whitehall.

It was during the nineteenth century that the art of the ship-carver reached its highest level, continuing its evolution in the merchant ship after its decay had set in in the Naval service, until it attained its perfection in those lovely figures that terminated the glorious sweeping lines of the swift clipper hulls. There was little else in the way of decoration on those austerely beautiful fabrics. Their builders knew better than to plaster them with ornamental barnacles. The eye followed the unerring sweep of their gracious lines to rest satisfied on the figure of knight or warrior, prince or chieftain or queen—the unsigned masterpiece of some nameless craftsman's skill.

And what a gallery was there ! There were allegorical figures of all sorts, like the " Lightning's " maiden grasping her golden thunderbolt. There was Friar Tuck in russet robe and Robin Hood in

Lincoln green. There were Jack Tars and John Chinamen. There were mandarins and rajahs and Red Indian chiefs with their feathers and war-paint. There were Arthurian knights and ladies—" Sir Lancelot " and " Guinevere." There were sprites and fairies—" Oberon," " Titania," " Ariel," " Undine." There were characters from Shakespeare —" Othello " and " Desdemona." There were characters from Scott—" Ivanhoe," " Cedric the Saxon," " Young Lochinvar," " Madge Wildfire," " Lord of the Isles," " Lady of the Lake." There were Maids of Judah and Maids of Athens. There were sailors, soldiers, generals, admirals, statesmen. There were heroes of antiquity, like Leonidas the Spartan, and heroes of modernity, like Kosciusko. There was " Tam o' Shanter " and the braw " Nannie." There were busts of Queen Victoria (where in those days was there *not* a bust of Queen Victoria ?), of Jenny Lind, of Florence Nightingale. There were portraits of somebodies and nobodies in side whiskers and stick-up collars. There were old skippers now long forgotten. There were gentlewomen with braided hair, like faded photographs in old albums. There were gipsy brides and witches on broomsticks. There were sea serpents and dragons, eagles and lions. There were women in flowing robes and there were women in the " altogether "—or there was at any rate one well-known example of the latter kind. That was the old

" Java," one of John Company's fleet, whose figurehead, a nude woman, was said to have a romantic story connected with it. A British officer, so the tale went, had rescued the daughter of an Indian prince from a tiger which had carried her off into the jungle while she was bathing, and to show his gratitude the father built the ship and presented it to the girl's rescuer—the figurehead being intended as a memorial of the deed. Whether there is anything in it or not I cannot say ; certainly the " Java " *had* such a figurehead, for Lieutenant Coates unearthed it among the ballast in the old ship when she was a hulk at Gibraltar in the 'nineties.

And now they are gone, nearly all of them ; vanished more completely than ancient Egypt or the toy of some Pompeian child, but for the few which still survey the altered world of shipping with the gaze, resigned yet melancholy, of a decayed aristocrat surveying the new régime. What has become of them all, the grotesque and the beautiful, the quaint and the bizarre ? Gone, gone . . . flickered away in salty flames on seaboard hearth-stones, driftwood and wreckage on the Seven Seas. A scattered remnant, battered, weatherworn, nose-less, linger in the gardens of coastguardsmen or outside fishermen's inns. A whole company bears witness under the Tresco palms to the efficacy of the natural defences of Scilly. But for the most part they are vanished and vanishing. Would it not be possible, one wonders, to preserve the few surviving examples of so ancient and lost a handicraft—if, indeed, one may not venture to call it an art?

CHAPTER IX

TWO RIVERS

King's Lynn and its Memories—A Nautical Friar—Captain George Vancouver—Lumber—A Troublesome Peer—A Barber of Ideas.

KING'S LYNN is one of those places you would never take for a seaport—especially if you see it first, as I did, on a market day, when it is full of straddling farmers in cords and leggings, and women with baskets, and carts with crates of hens, and whooping drovers, and hairy colts throwing their heels about in the side streets round the sale-ground. For it has to-day, as it has always had, " one foot on sea and one on land," and in these times it is perhaps the landward aspect which is the more conspicuous.

It is much too obvious to call Lynn quaint. For it really is so impossibly, so staggeringly—well, let us say " old-world," though that is perhaps no less obvious—and so unconsciously and naturally old-world. Places one calls quaint are generally more or less conscious of it. They wear their quaintness like a fancy dress. Every shop is a " shoppe,"

every tea room is " Ye Olde " something or other,
and is furnished with sham antiques and adorned
with art draperies. But for some reason Lynn has
escaped all that. It has grown old comfortably,
without being aware of it; and its bustle and
importance have slipped away from it and left it
to go to sleep comfortably. It doesn't seem to
brood over its departed splendours, but only to be
drowsing the hours away like some old retired
merchant captain with a bandanna over his nose.
Its old age has nothing melancholy about it; and
indeed Norfolk seems to be a county where age
seems to mellow rather than decay. Its octogen-
arians marry, and have families too. There was,
I believe, a famous Earl of Leicester who did so.

Lynn is a place of many associations, both
historical and literary. Vague reminiscences of
one's youthful excursions into history seem to
connect it with King John and the treasure which
he lost in the treacherous sands of the Wash. And
it was from Lynn, also, that the stern-faced men
set forth on the memorable occasion when Eugene
Aram walked between with gyves upon his wrists.
Unpleasant characters, both of them; I cannot
conceive why that commonplace criminal, the
usher-murderer, should have been allowed to trail
the memory of his sordid deed over the length and
breadth of England, nor why anybody should ever
have troubled to write a poem about him. He

presides, like some evil tutelary deity, over one of
the fairest spots in Yorkshire ; and here in Lynn
you meet him again.

But for me it is no such dark personality that
haunts the streets and wharves of the old city ;
nor is it even that venturesome Friar of the twelfth
century who tucked up his gown and went a-sea-
faring, to bring back a wondrous account of the
Maelstrom which, no doubt, everybody set down as
a prodigious cuffer. Neither is it Fanny Burney,
who spent some years of her girlhood here, and no
doubt found plenty to take in with her bright,
observant eyes.

The first time I was there—it was a day of grey,
stooping skies and bitter wind—I was looking for
such relics as time might have left of the sojourn
here of Captain George Vancouver, one of the lesser
naval stars whose names cluster around the central
planet, Nelson, in the constellation of Norfolk's
sea-greatness.

The East Anglian seaboard has bred sailors as
many and as fearless as those of Devon herself,
though for some reason it has missed its fair share
of popular fame. Sir Christopher Myngs, at whose
burial old seadogs wept honest tears, was a Norfolk
man, and a naval hero in times when British
prestige at sea was at a low ebb ; and so also was
Sir Cloudesley Shovel, the " hawsepipe " admiral,
the legend of whose tragic end still haunts the reefs

of Scilly. And not least among Norfolk's sons must
be accounted that naval officer who was Cook's
shipmate and successor, whose name goes down
through the ages linked with those of a great modern
seaport and of a noble island.

There is, alas ! very little but the memory remaining of the old house where George Vancouver was
born—an irony, perhaps, where so much has
survived the passage of the centuries. One little
half-timbered fragment with a tiled mansard roof
still stands, its crooked window looking out on to
the Quakers' meeting-house and its prim little yard ;
but the rest of the house is gone, and a new house,
one of the few new shops in Lynn, has been built
on its site. This is one of the parts where change
has been busy. But King Street and Queen Street,
and the narrow alleys which run down from them
to the river, and the Tuesday and the Saturday
market-places, are as if the years had stood still.
Their mansions with the tall crow-stepped gables
which look as if they might have been transported
bodily from the side of some Dutch canal, their
ancient archways with twisted Renaissance pillars
and carved stone faces peering out at you from
unexpected corners, their dark passages giving upon
paved courtyards and squares of garden built round
with antique houses, have not changed by so much
as a stone for centuries. There is an air of ghostly
powder and patches about the old Assembly Rooms,

THE CUSTOM HOUSE, KING'S LYNN

where a scene-painter now plies his calling; and
the memory of bygone hospitality lingers in the
great old houses where the merchants of Lynn
dwelt in princely pomp in the times when this
ranked fourth among all the ports of England. And
the little Custom House, with its cupola a-top and
the statue of the Merry Monarch in classic costume
over the door, has not altered since Vancouver's
father first drove a quill there.

His associations with Lynn would be the associations of boyhood. In those days a sailor's life
began early—at ten or eleven—and thereafter leave
came but seldom. No doubt had he lived he might
have returned to Lynn in the evening of his days.
It is a way Norfolk men have. But, like Cook, he
did not live to be old; he was only forty when he
died. But he had already written his name large
upon the map of the world.

I followed the slim shadow of the boy Vancouver
all through the quiet streets of the old town : by
the old wharves, where, no doubt, he found much
to delight the dreaming heart of an adventurous
boy in the days when the whalers still came in
from the Greenland fishery, and the ships from the
Baltic, and the bluff-bowed Dutchmen with wine
to fill the great cellars where the spiders spin their
webs to-day. And after all it was not in the old
town that I found him at last.

I had passed on to the cosy little docks—the child

of Lynn's old age, and, as such, greatly beloved—
where there was a steamer or two unloading, with
just such fair-haired, stocky Easterlings lounging
about their decks as Lynn has known since the
beginning of her history. The shrimping boats
were all in harbour, their tiny pennons fluttering
over the top of the high, tarred railing which
surrounds the " Fisher Fleet." And there were

> Tarry smells, and cockleshells,
> And tombstones all in a row. . . .

Tarry smells from the creosote works . . . and
cockleshells enough to furnish a garden for all the
Contrary Marys in the world and then some . . .
and tombstones imported ready-made from the
Continent, cold *hic jacets* and all complete, but for
a blank space for the name !

And then, suddenly, I smelt deals ! Deals—the
unforgettable, unmistakable, clean, pungent smell
of them—and lo ! I was thousands of miles away !

Gone the slow, turbid Ouse, melancholy under the
grey melancholy sky ; gone the ancient tower of
St. Nicholas Church, where dead-and-gone " pilots
of this town " sleep under its shadow beneath
weathered tombstones (not imported) ; gone the
Tuesday market with its big Georgian hotels, and
its Corn Exchange, and the grass growing between
its cobbles, and an assemblage of the most
ornate merry-go-rounds ever I saw in my life
(for Lynn, be it known, makes merry-go-rounds

for the world) getting ready for the great Lynn
Mart.

And instead there was the mighty Fraser, green
and brimming with the melting of the snows . . .
and the spars of a barque or two loading at the
lumber mill . . . and the chatter of the Chinese
firemen playing fan-tan on the forecastle head of a
Blue Funnel liner . . . and the mewing of the gulls,
back from their mating in the islands . . . and the
cosmopolitan crowds along Hastings Street . . .
and the rosy flush of the sunset flooding up the sky.
Or Victoria Harbour in the early morning, the mist
just rolling away from the straits, and Race Rocks,
and the far, white Olympic peaks . . . and the first
rays of the sun flashing on the gilded figure of
Captain George Vancouver on his dome, looking out
for ever across the seas he sailed and the islands he
claimed for England a century and more ago.

.   .   .   .   .

Captain Vancouver is one of our maritime worthies
of whom very little of a personal nature seems to be
known. There is, I believe, no authentic life of
him, and such information as is available is contained
in his own account of his voyages.

He was born at Lynn, as mentioned on a previous
page, in 1758, the son of a clerk in the Custom House
there. At thirteen he entered the Royal Navy as
a seaman. This, of course, does not imply that he

belonged to the " hawsepipe " officer category.   It
was quite a usual thing in the case of boys who
were waiting for a nomination as midshipman in a
ship which already carried her full complement of
junior officers.   Nelson, it will be remembered,
began his naval career with the technical rating of
officer's servant.

Young Vancouver sailed with Cook in the
" Resolution " as a seaman, and later as midshipman
in the " Discovery," so that he got the explorer
spirit into his blood early.   He was present at
Rodney's Battle of the Saints on April 12, 1782,
and a few years later he was commissioned to fit
out a ship then being built for the Admiralty by
Messrs. Randall for the purpose of exploring the
South Seas.   The South Sea expedition, however,
never came off.   The new ship, the " Discovery,"
as she was called, after Cook's famous vessel, was
diverted to another purpose.

Negotiations had been in progress between
England and Spain regarding the latter country's
occupation of the coast of Vancouver Island about
Nootka Sound, which had already been formally
claimed for Britain by Cook when he first discovered
it.   It fell to Vancouver's lot to proceed thither to
receive back the land which the Spaniards had
seized, and at the same time to explore the coasts
and seas to the northward, partly with a view to
discovering the sea passage from Behring Sea to

the Atlantic, in which opinion in England obstinately continued to believe.

He sailed in the new " Discovery " on March 8, 1791, touching at Australia on the way, where he explored part of the south-west coast, and visiting New Zealand, noting as a result on the map of the Dusky Bay district, where Cook had written " Nobody knows what," " Somebody knows what." Then he sailed north and carried through successfully his negotiations with the courtly Spaniard Quadra, whose name still survives on the street map of the city of Victoria.

Cook had believed Nootka Sound to be a part of the North American mainland, and it remained for Vancouver to circumnavigate for the first time the noble island which bears his name. And how difficult a task that was can hardly be realized by anyone who does not know those waters—hardly, even, by anyone who has plodded comfortably and safely in a steamer among the innumerable islands of the Strait of Juan de Fuca and the Gulf of Georgia, which Vancouver entered for the first time and named after his sovereign. There is, by the way, one example of Vancouver's christening which it is hard to excuse : that is Mount Baker, which was named after one of the members of the expedition. Surely so glorious a peak merited something more distinguished in the way of a name.

The voyage was not without its excitements,

9

quite apart from those attending navigation in strange waters. Among the ship's company was a certain crazy Cornish nobleman, Thomas Pitt, third Lord Camelford, then a young fellow of nineteen, who was later to attain a doubtful repute as a duellist. Such a character was not likely to take kindly to Naval discipline. His turbulent nature could not but get him into trouble. Vancouver had him put into the bilboes, flogged him three times, and at last, finding he could do no good with him, deposited him on the beach at Hawaii to find his way home as he could.

Camelford worked his passage home in a merchant ship, and on arrival in England sent his late commanding officer a challenge, which the latter quite rightly declined to accept unless some responsible person of higher rank than himself should consider that he had exceeded his disciplinary rights and owed the young peer satisfaction.

Sir Joseph Banks has recorded his opinion that Camelford had received exceedingly harsh and unjust treatment. The available evidence is somewhat conflicting. Banks was not a Naval man himself, and to judge by the difference of opinion which led him to part company from Cook he was inclined to be decidedly impatient of the ordinary rules governing matters of discipline.

The eccentric young Cornish nobleman was no doubt even more so. He had in him the makings

of a first-class mutineer and leader of mutineers ;
and mutiny in remote seas, like those to which
Vancouver's expedition was bound, was a very real
danger. The mutiny of the "Bounty" is a case
in point. Both Drake and Magellan had found it
harder to round Cape Treachery than Cape Horn.

Moreover, a man trained in Cook's school, while
he might be a strict disciplinarian, was not likely
to be a savage martinet. The benevolent expression
which marks Vancouver's portrait—reputed by
Lemuel Abbott—in the National Portrait Gallery
is, indeed, little to go by. He may have been one
of those skippers who was the soul of amiability
ashore and "a reg'lar old devil afloat"! But there
seems no reason to think so in his case. Camelford's
subsequent career shows him to have been vain and
hot-tempered to the point of insanity, and he must
have been a constant annoyance and danger to such
an expedition as Vancouver's.

. . . . .

One ought not to part company from Lynn
without mentioning still another of her marine
notabilities, though of quite a different kind.

You would hardly on the face of it connect a
barber with the sea, otherwise than as a participator
in the time-honoured ceremonies observed on
crossing the Line. But our Lynn celebrity was a
barber, Thomas Hamblin by name, who in a manner

of speaking got his dash of salt water by marriage, his wife being the daughter of a Lynn pilot. This Thomas Hamblin it was who, in the early years of the eighteenth century, was the first to give practical effect to the idea of a lightship. He, with his partner Avery—not the gentleman who shared the lurid reputation of Teach and Morgan and Bartholomew Roberts and the rest of the merry company of pirates and buccaneers—secured from the Trinity House a licence enabling them to establish a lightvessel on the Nore Sand and to levy dues upon passing shipping for its support. Unfortunately for themselves, the partners demanded such high dues that shipmasters and merchants began to complain, and the news of the rich harvest they were reaping came to the ears of the Trinity Brethren. Accordingly their licence was withdrawn, a yearly payment being made to them for a stated time in consideration of the expense which they had already incurred in establishing the light. And the barber of Lynn had " lighted a candle which has never been put out ! "

CHAPTER X

NELSON'S COUNTRY

THE seaboard of Norfolk is in many respects the exact antithesis of that of Cornwall or of Devon—perhaps nowhere more strikingly so than in the relation one to another of the sea and the shore.

In the West Country it is largely in the sharpness of its contrasts that the charm of the coast scenery consists, so that at one moment, as it were, you are looking upon a rugged and rockbound shore where the sound of the tide is never silent and the next you are in some "island valley of Avilion" out of sight and sound of the sea. The land goes rioting down to the very water's edge in all its laughing luxuriance of tree and fern and flower; and the salt waves that hide the bones of a hundred wrecked ships mingle their sharp savour with the sweetness of April orchards and hedges white with May foam.

But in the East Country, Nelson's country, it is different. The sea and the land are less definitely assigned to their several rulers. The land and the sea are indeed perpetually at war—invading con-

tinually each other's marches so that one might
be hard put to it, at times to say which is the
conqueror. Here, churches, farms, villages, the
very graves of the dead, lie buried beneath the
champing and the tramplings of the victorious
chariots of the tides. There, the wiry marram
grass, with its sinewy, clutching fingers, clings
jealously to the soil of dykes which guard the salty
pastures laboriously won from the sea.

You may know the sea for your neighbour by
many tokens : by the trees that shudder shore-
wards in patient endurance of the rude buffetings
of the North Sea gales—by the crowds of gulls that
miles inland whiten the farmer's furrow as he plods
his stubborn clayey acres—by the air, full, bracing,
and buoyant, that shepherds the cloud-shadows
across the broad breast of the countryside, or drives
the low misty rack before it from the sea. The
trees are mostly such sturdy growths as can best
survive storms and hard winters and late, unkind
springs. No primroses lift their pale, delicate faces
to front the bleak East Anglian April. No steep
lanes frame in their tangles of honeysuckle and wild
rose glimpses of sea blue beyond all believing.
No nightingales sing in the June copses. But
the English blackbird, the English throstle flute
year in, year out from their native oak and
thorn.

It is a land, on the whole, of controlled tones, of

colouring rather subdued than brilliant : a stern
land, a reticent land, a land as essentially English
as its inhabitants. I have said " English," because
there is, I suppose, less of the Celt remaining hereabouts than in any other part of these islands.
The Norfolk man is cold, stolid, matter-of-fact,
perhaps a thought lacking in imagination. He
comes of Danish and Anglo-Saxon stock, with
possibly a dash of the Fleming. He calls himself
—not without a comfortable content in the appella-
tion—a " Norfolk dumplen."

And these same " Norfolk dumplens," as we have
seen, have set their mark on history. They are a
seafaring people—but, in the true Norse tradition,
they are farmers as well. They drive the plough,
and the salt fret in their veins calls them from it
to the shifting furrows of the sea. They follow the
sea, and the thought of their stiff Norfolk soil is
with them the world over. They come back to
Norfolk to farm when their sailoring days are over,
and live as close to the sea as they may without
actually wetting their feet when they go out of
doors, with a boat or two somewhere around to
potter about with when the salt water yearning
comes over them.

Their villages are bleak, four-square, small-
windowed, built to withstand heavy weather,
standing up to face the gales like sailors with feet
planted firm on a slanting deck. They have (or

had) a reputation as wreckers equal to that of the
Cornishmen. " Good night, father, good night,
mother ! God send a ship ashore afore mornin' ! "
—so, the saying goes, went the child's nightly
prayer in the days gone by.

And, good sooth, the prayer was often answered !
Of all the coasts which have taken toll of the ships
of Britain, this has claimed the most. If one
glances at a wreck chart of the British Isles in, say,
the 'sixties, it is not the Manacles nor the Lizard,
not the Wolf nor the Bishop, where the wreck-marks
crowd the closest. It is on the east coast, where
the land goes shoaling out into the sea with a
hundred hidden sandbanks and vicious tiderips,
that the map is black with them, and that the lost
ships lie one upon another, like coffins in an ancient
graveyard.

It might well seem to the stranger matter for
comment that to the greatest of all her sons Norfolk
should have set up no worthy monument. Nelson's
own village of Burnham Thorpe shows, indeed,
some few local memorials—a pulpit, a bust, a village
institute—such as might with an equal fitness com-
memorate some worthy, undistinguished country
squire or parson. But for the rest there is little
material to remind those who go there—" This
place knew Nelson." The very house where he was
born is gone : it fell down, or was pulled down,
some fifty years ago. And the tower which domin-

ates the countryside was erected to the memory of a Norfolk farmer.

And yet there was nothing typical about Norfolk's most famous sailor. He was no more typical of Norfolk than he was typical of England.

The Duke of Wellington—for all his Irish birth—had the failings and the virtues that are essentially English ; among the former the rather narrow outlook, the dread of its own innate sentimentality that takes refuge in an exaggerated self-repression. Drake was the very embodiment of the Tudor spirit of adventure. But Nelson was Nelson ! He was the keen blade forged for its own destined purpose, on the anvil of that fate which some would have us think blind. " There is but one Nelson," said old Lord St. Vincent. His lambent genius had about it a quality almost other-worldly. He was a poet made sailor, and his victories have for all time a rhythm and a swing like a Border ballad.

So that, after all, the instinct which has refrained from the attempt to capture in bricks and mortar the memory of that living flame which was the genius of Nelson is perhaps a right one. Such monuments rather obscure than illumine a great name. They are like trumpery vases on a stone altar to the Unknown God. There is a certain fine simplicity about that inn sign of " The Hero " one

meets with hereabouts, over the doors of little inns
where no doubt a century ago men drank down their
British beer and blessed the name of Nelson because
they drank it in freedom. It is the simplicity of
which only the unlettered and the wise are capable ;
and how right it is may be seen by the contrast
between the first inscription on the slab in Westminster Abbey which marks the grave of the
Unknown Soldier and the wordy rhodomontade
with which an unhappy second thought has
replaced it.

> What needs our Nelson for his honoured bones
> The labours of an age in piled stones.

His memorial is all round us. It is the free land,
the free seas he left us. *Si monumentum requiris—*
the tag could nowhere be more aptly quoted. It is
there, there . . . a confused multitudinous shouting
beyond the line of the sand dunes . . . a pale band
of grey under the stooping sky . . . a mingling of
blown spume and driven sand when the north-easter
blows.

The sea is leaving this part of the coast. But
still, when the tide is high and the wind at its back,
it comes flooding in again through the silted channels,
lipping the mouldering wharves, the deserted
staithes, where the desolate winds whistle in the
disused maltings, the stranded wrecks sunk deep in
piled sand . . . flooding the rabbits from their

burrows, the birds from their nests in the
sea lavender . . . wooing the land afresh with
its salt kisses, like the ghost of a lost passion
renewed in dreams . . . the sea that called
Nelson. . . .

SHIP MODELS

IT is a strange thing—though perhaps characteristic of the odd national indifference of this
people towards its sea history—that the capital
city and the principal seaport of a great maritime
power should possess no museum specially devoted
to the service to which it owes its prosperity and
its very existence.

There are, it is true, quite a number of notable
collections of ship models and other nautical relics
scattered about the metropolis, to be found by those
who know where to look for them. There are some
in the Royal United Service Institution, some at
Greenwich, some at Trinity House. The Sailors'
Home in Well Street possesses several, one or two
of which look like exceptionally good ones whose
history would be worth tracing. Some fine builders'
models of ships built at Blackwall Yard are in
the Poplar Library. And there is, of course, the

extensive collection in the Science and Art Museum at South Kensington.

But in most cases they are, so to speak, side-issues. There is in all London no museum, no gallery, devoted simply and solely to matters of the sea, like that at Amsterdam and at Venice and in certain American cities.

There would, no doubt, be considerable difficulties to overcome in forming such a collection—not least that of housing it when formed. But they ought not to be insurmountable. Perhaps one day the ancient London Company of Shipwrights, which has been enjoying the temporary hospitality of the Apothecaries ever since its original home was destroyed in the Great Fire, may have a hall of its own again ; and should that day come, what better home could be desired for a maritime museum ?

Such an institution would collect, house, catalogue, and render accessible to the public authentic models of the famous ships of old time, showing the development of the merchant ship from the earliest days of seaborne trade—models of East Indiamen, of tea clippers, of wool clippers, of wooden ships, composites, iron ships, and steel ships ; models of ships intended for special trades, such as whaling or salvage or cable-laying. It should include not only builders' models and half models, but good examples of the sailors' models, which in many cases are the only contemporary representations of the ships they reproduce ; not forgetting the humble " bottled ship," the making of which was once the favourite diversion of the shellback's " watch below."

Many such models—part of the historical inheritance of the nation, and priceless to the nautical chronicler of the future—are being lost every year through neglect or through sheer ignorance of their existence, handed over to children as playthings, or left to moulder in forgotten lumber-rooms or seldom-entered cellars of old shipbuilding concerns, while an even larger number are going out of the country as a result of the boom in model-collecting on the other side of the Atlantic.

In the nautical museum should also be brought together contemporary pictures and prints of the ships of bygone days, and perhaps such examples as still remain of the lost art of the figurehead carver. Relics of ships specially noted for any reason might well be included, such as the " River Clyde " and the " Brussels," and vessels famed in the annals of Arctic and Antarctic exploration. And, last but not least, here should be preserved those old ships' logs whose yellowed pages preserve in their curt, sailorlike entries more of the eternal verities of the sea than may be gathered from volumes of polished and self-conscious prose.

.   .   .   .   .

Apart from public institutions, there are a number of noteworthy private collections in this country, and among these probably the finest since the Cuckfield collection crossed the Atlantic is that belonging to Commander Fry, of the training ship " Mercury." It could have no more appropriate home than the shore of Hamble Creek—the scene of the first naval victory in English history, the cradle of the Tudor Navy, and the place which has seen so many boys brought up to fear God, honour the King, and do their duty as seamen and Britons in the Navy and the Mercantile Marine.

One of the special treasures of the collection is a magnificent model in frame of the " Prince Royal," built in 1640, with a prancing equestrian figurehead of King Charles the First, carved and gilded. It calls to mind the well-known picture " A Whip for Van Tromp," for this ship, built from the designs of the famous master shipwright Peter Pett, was a notable fighter in the Dutch wars of the seventeenth century, at which time (the Commonwealth being in power) she was known as the " Resolution."

King Charles the Second, whatever his faults as a husband and as a king, had at any rate the redeeming point that he took a keen interest in his Navy. He it was who first introduced yachts into this country, and he had several built at the Royal

dockyards, amongst them one which he called
" Old Fubbs," the nickname of the reigning favourite, the Duchess of Portsmouth. There is a very
ornate model of one of these yachts—it may have
been this very " Old Fubbs "—in the " Mercury "
collection, all carved cherubs and roses, garlands
and scrolls and chubby loves, in the florid style of
the Restoration period.

Then there is a beautiful rigged model of H.M.S.
" Tartar," which, built at Deptford in 1734, was
renowned twenty years later as a veritable tartar
among the Channel privateers. She is a tiny ship,
only about eighteen inches long, but she is perfect
in every particular, with her fierce Tartar figurehead
and twenty-two brass guns. Her rigging is interesting, showing the lateen yard on the mizen in use
at that time.

Very few models of that period have the original
rigging still in position. Such slender and delicate
fabrics naturally perish very quickly if exposed to
the air, and fall into an unrecognizable tangle, and
hence the greater number of the rigged specimens
in museums have been re-rigged (possibly more than
once) by experts, with the help of contemporary
evidence, and to a certain extent from guesswork.

A very pretty model of a sixty-four once belonged
to Lord Nelson. It was formerly believed to
represent H.M.S. " Ruby," but there are several

indications, apart from her general lines, that she is of French origin, especially the fleur-de-lis device which occurs very frequently among her rather elaborate decorations. She was most probably a prize, and is possibly the " Solitaire," a French sixty-four captured by the " Ruby " in the West Indies in 1782.

I don't think I ever saw a prettier little box of tricks than the model of the Dutch ship " Washington," built in 1797, the flagship of Vice-Admiral Storey in 1798–99, which after her capture by Mitchell's squadron in the Vlieter served in the British Navy as the " Princess of Orange." The whole thing takes to pieces, and there is a numbered key to it in Dutch. The upper deck lifts off, revealing the interior, and still more sections may then be lifted out, showing the magazines, holds, and lamp-rooms—a marvel of patient and precise workmanship.

Then there is the French " Revolutionnaire," which was captured by four British frigates only a few weeks after she was launched. She was yet another example of the *sic vos non vobis* principle by which our Naval designers of the Napoleonic period reaped the harvest of the industry and enterprise of the French shipwrights ! She marked a great advance in several respects on previous ships of her class, and after her capture served as a useful pattern to later British builders.

10

The " Mordaunt " is an exceptionally fine model of an interesting ship, originally built for Lord Mordaunt, later Earl of Peterborough, for privateering purposes, and bought into the Royal service to prevent her being used against a friendly power. She is richly adorned in the fashion of the period, with cupids riding dolphins, lions and coats-of-arms, that of her original owner among them.

There is also a square-rigged ketch in the collection which is, I believe, unique. To us, of course, a ketch stands for a fore-and-aft rig ; but ketches of this square-rigged type were very much used as bomb and despatch vessels during the eighteenth century, and they were also favoured by the buccaneers, which may be taken as pretty sound evidence that they must have been handy little ships with a good turn of speed.

    .   .   .   .   .

There have always been a certain number of people—from Mr. Pepys onwards—who have collected builders' models. But it is only during the last few years that the ordinary sailor's model—the pleasure model, so to speak—has become sought after by dealers and collectors.

The builder's model stands in a class by itself. It differs in several important respects from the

type just mentioned. It was made for a specific
purpose. It was meant to be

> to the larger plan
> What the child is to the man,
> Its counterpart in miniature :
> That with a hand more swift and sure
> The greater labour might be wrought. . . .

And also in the case of the elaborate unrigged
models of the Stuart ships the model was intended to be laid before the King's advisers for
approval.

These ornate little structures seem to have
gone out with the eighteenth century. No such
models were ever made of the later Blackwall-built
ships or of the wooden clippers. If they were, what
has become of them ? The paucity of ship models
of that period—even the ordinary half-model, which
is of little interest to any but experts—rather seems
to suggest that they were not preserved. There
may have been a reason. There was a great deal
of rivalry between shipbuilding firms in those days,
and steps may have been taken to ensure that the
models of new ships did not fall into the hands of
those who might thus get hold of secrets of design
and construction. But probably few models were
made at all, and drawings took their place very
largely in the shipyards of the nineteenth century.

The builder's model came before the actual ship—

the latter might, indeed, differ from it to some extent in detail. What may be classified as ornamental models are, on the other hand, miniature representations of ships already in existence. They cover a very wide field both of subject and of execution. Some are the work of men with a considerable knowledge of ship construction and sufficient mathematical skill to be able to make a scale model. Some are the clumsy efforts of Foc's'le Jack to reproduce to his liking some ship specially loved and admired. The first class may be almost equal to a builder's model in accuracy ; the second in many cases are the merest caricatures of the ships they are meant to portray.

I once tramped through endless, dreary Canning Town streets in quest of a model of a famous clipper ship, the work of a master rigger. I ran it to earth at last. A lachrymose lady with a sniff, who had apparently recently partaken of onions and a cup o' tea which kep' repeatin' on her somethink chronic, tried to sell it to me in a mixed lot with a solid mayogany table of the mid-Victorian period, a remnant of vanished glories in the public-'ouse business upon which she dilated with much verbosity and many hiccups.

Such a thing ! The dining table couldn't have been much more unlike a ship . . . rough and clumsy, with a ridiculous tuft of grey wool coming out of the galley stove-pipe, and impossibly lofty masts, and a lumpy hull whose deficiencies were partially concealed by a remarkably choppy paint sea.

And she thought—poor soul!—it was worth twenty-five pounds!

The fact is that the same thing is happening with regard to ship models that has happened about old furniture. Things have gone from one extreme to another. People are asking—and, what is more, they are getting—as many pounds as they were getting shillings a few years back.

Twenty years ago nearly every sailor made models of a sort. Sailors are fond of such tiny toys. It was, I believe, Hendrick Hudson the explorer who always kept a model ship in his cabin, with a crew of tame mice that he taught to run about its rigging.

I know of one which has been more than a century in the making. It represents the three-decker " Achilles "—or rather, I imagine, the " Achille " —which played so brilliant a part in the lee line at Trafalgar, which made short work of the " Montanez " and the " Argonauta," and whose log records, " Hove overboard sixty-seven butts to make room in the forehold for the prisoners " from the sinking " Berwick."

The model was begun by the great-uncle of the present owner, who lost a leg while serving on board its original. He died when the hull was still unfinished, and it passed into the possession of a brother, who carried it a stage farther before he too died, leaving it to his son.

The son did nothing to it, and a great-nephew of the veteran—a well-known commander of clipper ships—put the finishing touches on her a hundred years and more after her keel had been laid. Probably very few little ships have so long and so authentic a history.

. . . . .

I went on board a little French ship in the Surrey Docks not long ago and had the offer of a couple of pretty little models, one of the " La France " under full sail, the other of the ship herself (her name I have quite forgotten). They were nice little things and I was tempted to buy them. But their paper sails would soon have lost their freshness without a glass case. Besides which, they were not full models, only those rather whited sepulchre-like affairs with hulls like the faces of Hans Andersen's Trolls. Still, I have regretted them since, and I may come to regret them more. Makers of models of any sort grow fewer every year.

The French have always excelled as model makers. There are perhaps no finer examples of the art than those so-called " ivory "—really bone—ships made by French prisoners during the Napoleonic wars.

They are masterpieces of delicate and careful handi-
work, and the carving has all the detail and the
loving finish of an old Chinese ivory.

They were made, of course, partly no doubt to
while away time, but also with a view to selling
them and so eking out the scanty rations of the
prisoners and replenishing their wardrobes. The
probability is that they were not in any case the
work of one man, but a sort of co-operative venture.
The war prisons contained a great variety of ranks
and occupations. One man would draw the plans
and work out the scale, another would undertake
the rigging, and so forth, and the actual carving
was probably executed by Breton jet workers, large
numbers of whom were serving in the French
Navy.

There is a lovely big one of the fighting
" Temeraire " in the Southampton Museum that I
could gaze at for hours—a real " queen's dolls'
house " of a ship. Every detail is there, and
everything is to scale. The tiny blocks, the rails,
the anchor, the catheads, the capstan—nothing is
forgotten ; and there is the tiniest and most beautiful of carving in all sorts of places where it is hardly
seen—on the fighting tops and the forecastle
bulwarks. Many a sigh went to the making of
that lovely thing, no doubt. I hope those who had
a hand in it got back safe to their beloved France
in the end, and that it was not written of them, as

it is of one of their compatriots in a Hampshire graveyard,

> He was a prisoner of war.
> But death has set him free.

. . . . .

There is a certain sentimental appeal even about the poorest of sailors' models. They represent the striving after self-expression of those to whom such utterance was a thing infinitely more painful and difficult than the most difficult and painful of bodily effort and physical endurance. They are a groping after that vision, that ideal without which in some form man's life is but a living death. And by however much they fall short of that ideal its light has shone upon them for a moment, and given them a soul.

. . . . .

And now for just a few words about those " bottled ships," the making of which was a favourite dog-watch diversion with so many old shellbacks of twenty or thirty years ago. I mean, of course, bottled sailing ships. I have seen steamers in bottles, but they are a mere travesty of the real thing.

The real ship in a bottle is a sailing vessel, and she may be either under sail or at anchor. And the bigger the ship in proportion to the bottle the

better, since the puzzle thus appears all the greater
to the uninitiated : How did the ship get into the
bottle ?

The solution is really quite simple. It is the
exact opposite of the answer to the rather
similar poser : "How did the apple get into the
dumpling ?"

The bottle was *not* made round the ship. A
glass-blowing apparatus does not form part of the
usual apparatus of a ship's forecastle. Nor was
the bottom removed and then replaced by some
mysterious method.

No ! the ship got in by the usual entry and exit
in the case of a bottle—by the neck. And this is
how it is done.

First you must get your bottle. A whisky bottle
is the kind most frequently used, perhaps because
it is the kind most easily to be obtained from the
steward. But any bottle will do so long as it is
made of clear glass. I once saw a lovely little
ship in a tiny flat bottle, such as is used for small
quantities of glycerine or castor oil, and the
bottle was so full of the ship that it was really
hard to believe that it had got in through the
neck.

The hull comes next, and this must be made of a
size to go through the neck of the bottle, leaving a
little margin. The masts are fixed on pins so that
they will lie down flat with the hull. The yards

are similarly arranged, so that they will cockbill parallel with the masts, so that the whole thing folds up like an umbrella.

The time has now arrived when the ship is to be put into the bottle, the lower half of which has been filled with paint to represent the sea, with sometimes a well-known lighthouse in the background, or a representation of some port at home or abroad if the ship is to be at anchor.

This is decidedly a ticklish business. No matter how flat the masts and yards lie, the navigation of " Bottleneck Passage " has splintered the spars of many a gallant little ship, not to mention making the dog-watch hideous with the imprecations of the baffled shipwright.

When the ship is safely in the bottle, the masts are pulled up and the yards squared by means of the surplus thread left for the purpose. This is then burnt off or (if the ship is shown at anchor) rove through the hawsepipe and carried down into the " sea." The cork is put in and sealed, and your bottled ship is complete.

I have in a bottle a little full-rigger painted grey, with black bulwarks and painted ports. She is flying the pilot Jack at the fore, a burgee at the main with the name " Julia " on one side and " Lewis " on the other, and a red swallow-tail— evidently a house flag—at the mizen, with a white black-centred star in the middle.

I have never been able to trace her flag or find out anything about her. What was her history, I wonder ? What voyages did she make, what storms did she weather ? Was her luck good or bad, were her captains bold or cautious ? And what forgotten old shellback put her likeness in a bottle in golden dog-watches of long ago, to endure when her soaring masts, her stout spars, all the beauty and strength and swiftness that were hers are gone down into oblivion for ever ?

. . . . .

As with ships' models, so it is with ship pictures. Contemporary portraits of the sailing vessels of the past, no matter how negligible their artistic merits, have suddenly attained a certain value in the eyes of collectors.

It is a strange thing how few pictures of ships we possess which have both high artistic value and technical correctness. There are, of course, two or three famous Turners (I *have* heard hypercritical mariners find fault with " The Fighting Temeraire " because you can't see the tow-rope !), and there are a good number by Copley Fielding, and there are all those beautiful etchings by E. W. Cooke, R.A., which, with their wealth of detail, provide such valuable evidence regarding the ships of his period. Then, to come to more modern times, there are pictures by Clarkson Stanfield and Wyllie and

Napier Hemy and Bernard Gribble, and there is Somerscales' "Off Valparaiso," one of the very few famous sea pictures painted by a sailor, or a man who had been a sailor. And even in this, curiously enough, there is a technical point which troubles the nautical critic considerably. It will be noticed that one of the headsails—the one which is being hauled down—is filling out to port, the other to starboard, the wind being on the port quarter, or rather almost dead aft. The artist *may* be quite right; indeed, one would hardly expect him to be wrong on such a point. But those headsails worry the old shellback a whole lot.

Had there ever been a Morland or a Constable at sea what a boon would have been conferred on posterity; or had anyone depicted life on board ship with brush or pencil as Falconer depicted it in words! It is, when one comes to think of it, astonishing that at the very height and heyday of sail no one was found to immortalize the fleeting glory of the clipper ship. Artists go to the docks nowadays to paint the faded remnants of that noble epoch, but how many went when the docks were full of its splendours? No one ever painted the wool fleet in the South West India Dock. No one captured the grace and beauty of a tea clipper under sail, to delight the eyes of men when the ship herself was no more. And all that wealth of lovely line, of light and shade, of form and colour and movement, remained, on the whole, unrecorded save in the poor, halting, lame attempts of men whose power of execution lagged far behind their soaring vision.

Who knows them not, those formal ship pictures, with every sail standing out hard and stiff as a board, every reef-point clearly shown, every block put in accurately, nothing to which the most fault-finding mate could possibly take exception! Then the sea with its neat, regular waves, of a consistency somewhat resembling the sailor's idea of what pea-soup *ought* to be like! None of your blooming artistic untidiness here! Everything shipshape and Blackwall fashion, from truck to keelson, from the flag on the approaching pilot boat to Tuskar Light in the offing. . . .

Some of them are those turned out to order by artistic hacks for shipowners. Others are the work of the tame artists some ship-chandlers used to keep on tap, and the Chinese ship picture comes under this heading. But the greater number were painted by sailors themselves—on odd bits of boards, sometimes on tin, very often inside the lid of a sea-chest.

And some of those amateurs made an uncommonly good fist at it, as sailors have a way of doing at all sorts of jobs they take a fancy to tackle. I heard once of a skipper who made rather *too* good a job of one of his paintings. His ship (she was one

of the later wool clippers) had been through one
of those "northers" which are so unpleasant a
local weather phenomenon on the nitrate coast,
and the captain, when it was all over, took up his
brush and painted a picture of it—the sea, of course,
like a boiling pot, and all the anchored ships bobbing
up and down at their moorings like so many corks ;
one or two adrift, and driving down helplessly on
to the next ship in the tier.

When he arrived in Liverpool one of the members
of Lloyd's in that port came on board, and took a
great fancy to the picture. If fact, he was so much
taken with it that he asked if he might have it to
hang up in Lloyd's Room.

A few days later the skipper saw the same man
again.

"Oh, I say, Captain," he said, "I wonder if
you'd mind having that picture back again ? "

"What's the matter with the picture ? " asked
the captain, rather taken aback.

"Oh, nothing's the matter with the *picture*,"
said the other hastily ; "it's a capital picture.
The only thing is it's too realistic. Under-
writers here had no idea Valparaiso was such a
dangerous anchorage, and it's had the effect of
sending rates up with a jump ! "

Good and bad alike, these sailors' pictures have
the one great merit—sincerity. And since nothing
which is sincere can be wholly worthless, there shines

through them, in spite of the clumsy, faulty execution, something of the spirit of beauty which inspired them, some faint shadow and semblance of the lovely image the hand tried vainly to capture.

CHAPTER XII

TRINITY HOUSE AND ITS ASSOCIATIONS

A Georgian Interior—Trinity House Treasures—The " Loyal London "—The Church of St. Olave—Mr. Pepys and the Plague —New Castell Coal—Some " Geordie " Yarns.

TRINITY HOUSE is very much over-shadowed nowadays by the huge bulk of the Port of London building. It is a pity. These big modern buildings seem to have such a way of eclipsing, so far as size is concerned, their architectural surroundings. There is that immense Bush House, for instance, like a vast extinguisher all ready to be popped on the top of the little spire of Wren's St. Mary le Strand ; and the dome of the Central Hall, which looks so self-assertive and incongruous beside the ancient towers of Westminster.

And yet, for all their bigness, these lesser neighbours have a dignity which is denied to them ; for they are marked (even when they are not architectural masterpieces) by a sense of fine proportion which our age seems somehow to have hopelessly lost. Perhaps it is something to do with the size of our bricks and our stones. Perhaps it is fireproof construction. I don't know. But whatever the reason, the fact remains that the eye can rest with far greater satisfaction on the quiet little façade of Trinity House than on that of its more pretentious neighbour, with its great sprawling Neptunes and its brawny female clutching a ship's wheel as if she had just pulled it up by the roots. And there you have another example of the curious indifference of the British people to correctness in matters maritime. Why, in the name of all that is sensible, could not whoever designed that preposterous woman have made her hold her wheel more or less properly ? The wooden sailor on the top of a shipchandler's in the West India Dock Road would have looked better there than she does !

There is, on the other hand, nothing to complain about in the jolly little sea urchins, or whatever they are, dangling anchors along the front of Trinity House. They are as obviously fanciful as the lady with the steering wheel is solidly material, and ought to be in consequence technically correct.

The whole air of Trinity House is one of comfortable Georgian repose. It has a prim little paved court behind old iron railings, and a decorous pillared façade adorned with busts of King George and Queen Charlotte, as well as the cherubs with anchors, and the arms of Trinity House in stone,

11

the St. George's cross and the four ships, just as they may be seen on the Trinity flag at the present day.

And the atmosphere is not dispelled when you cross the threshold. There is no place in London quite like the Trinity House. It has none of the deadly, formal oppressiveness of an official building. It is called a house, and it is like a house—a house of the Georgian times which has never altered, where time has stood still; so that it is hard to believe that those are really the feverish, bustling hours of the twentieth century that are being numbered by the many unerring clocks which are one of the features of the place. One of these same clocks, by the way, stood for years in a lighthouse—I think the Bishop—where the seas and winds sometimes made the lofty structure (built of stones cunningly locked together, and fitting so closely that no mortar or cement need be used) tremble and sway so that crockery would fall from the shelves. What a change from the incessant thunder of the sea to this peaceful interior, these pleasant, cool, lofty rooms with their gleaming mahogany and walnut furniture, most of which was made in the house at the time it was built.

There are Chippendale chairs by the dozen, enough to make any collector green with envy. There are Sheraton settees and side-tables, there are dignified ranges of mahogany bookshelves as

PHIL. W. SMITH 1924

TRINITY HOUSE

old as the walls. And when a full-dress dinner is on foot there is a display of some of the finest goldsmiths' and silversmiths' work in London, including two magnificent sixteenth-century salvers and a couple of rare " steeple " loving-cups whose equals it would be very hard to find anywhere.

The walls are hung with old nautical prints and pictures, and the portraits of Trinity Masters and Brethren from the days of the Tudors and Stuarts onwards, bluff old seadogs for the most part, with here and there the smoother lineaments of some statesman or politician made an Elder Brother or Master *honoris causa*. There are a couple of Sir Joshuas ; one represents that Earl of Sandwich who was known in his day by the uncomplimentary nickname of " Jemmy Twitcher," and remembered to-day by the least questionable act of his public career—the invention of the sandwich. The portrait of Lord Howe—" Black Dick "—was formerly believed to be by Gainsborough, but later investigations have proved it to be by Gainsborough's nephew and pupil, Gainsborough Dupont, as also the big group of the Trinity Brethren of the period. An interesting point about the latter picture is that one of the figures—that at the extreme right of the canvas—has been added as a sort of postscript. He received his appointment after the picture was finished, and had to be tacked on afterwards. Another noteworthy portrait is that of

Sir John Leake, the boom-breaker of Derry, whose acquaintance has been already made in connexion with Old Stepney Church.

That of Pepys the diarist is a copy from the original painting. Pepys was, of course, connected not with the present house but with its grandfather, which stood in Water Lane, off Lower Thames Street, near the Custom House, on a site which still bears the name of Trinity Chambers. The next Trinity House was built in 1708, and, if contemporary testimony is to be believed, a very poor affair it was. In 1793-95 the present house was erected in its stead, to the designs of Samuel Wyatt; and among its notable features—whether accidental or not will never be known—is a large room which is one of the best in London from the after-dinner speaker's point of view. Every word uttered in an ordinary speaking voice can be heard from one end of the room to the other.

I suppose most of the great English statesmen of the last century have spoken in that room at one time or another, as well as many of the foreign kings and princes who have visited London during that time. And here it may be mentioned that probably many people have seen the full-dress uniform of Trinity House without knowing it. It is a particularly handsome and effective get-up, and is not infrequently sported by political and other celebrities who have been admitted Elder

Brethren without having any connexion with the sea. But they like wearing the uniform!

There are relics of Drake and autographs of Charles the Second and of Oliver Cromwell. There are a pair of ancient globes presented by a Stuart Admiral. There are models of lighthouses and lightships, among them the three Eddystone lighthouses, Winstanley's, Smeaton's, and the existing light. There are rare old charts of the sixteenth century. And last, but by no means least, there is what is perhaps the special pride of the place—the contemporary model of the "Loyal London," presented to Trinity House in 1674 or thereabouts by Sir Jeremy Smith, an Elder Brother who had previously commanded the ship in question.

This was long believed to be one of three ships— the "Royal William," the "Soveraigne of the Seas," or the "Britannia"; but its identity with the "Loyal London" has recently been definitely established. This ship was the gift of the City of London to the King. She was a three-decker, carrying ninety-six guns, and had a brief career, which was ended by her being burnt by the Dutch when they raided the Medway.

Her beautifully carved stern shows the Royal Arms, with those of Sir Jeremy Smith beneath. The model is a perfect piece of workmanship, and the hull being in frame only, without the planking, shows the seventeenth-century method of construction in every detail. But the great point about this model is that it is rigged, and, moreover, that the rigging is contemporary. She has grown old in the place, like everything about it. If a rope has shown signs of perishing, it has been replaced, but that is all. There has been none of that ill-advised re-rigging which has spoiled so many fine examples of old models. Consequently, she is to all intents and purposes just as she was when she was built under the instructions of, if not by, Jonas Shish, the Deptford chief shipwright, over a couple of hundred years ago.

.　　　.　　　.　　　.　　　.

It is strange to reflect that, for all its air of comfortable leisure, Trinity House is the centre of a vast and unsleeping system which embraces the whole of the pilotage and the lighting of the English coasts.

It is connected as it were by a thousand invisible threads with lonely rocks and reefs, with treacherous sandbanks and hidden shoals, with tiderips and channels and desolate bird-haunted islands ; with the light winking in and out the night through on some dancing buoy that marks a sunken rock, with the wheeling blade of light that swings its wide arc among the stars from the Wolf and the Eddystone and the Bishop. It links up the Lizard on its promontory, with the Maplin standing up on its spidery legs above the Thames Estuary ; with a hundred capes from Dungeness to the Longstone, from Walney to the North Foreland. It speeds by proxy every foreign-going ship that leaves our shores, and greets every new-comer from the farthest seas.

Certain of its ancient duties are no doubt honoured more in the breach than the observance. I don't think it is any longer part of the business of Trinity House to regulate the language, or the habits as regards temperance, of the British seaman ! It was so at one time. Every mariner who swore, cursed, or blasphemed on board ship had by the rules of Trinity House to pay a fine of one shilling to the ship's poor-box. So had every mariner who got drunk ! If the regulations were ever enforced there must have been a great many shillings collected, but it is more likely that the system was given up as a bad job. It has certainly lapsed now. One of the former powers of Trinity House might with advantage be revived—that of preventing foreigners serving in British ships, except by special licence.

As you pass out into the twentieth century again, just for a moment the river breeze that tosses the trees in the Tower garden, where many a fair and noble, many a sinful and innocent head rolled in the bloody dust of Tower Hill, and the far roar of the city traffic, seem like the thunder of the distant tide, the remote sighing of the tide on a rockbound shore. . . .

·   ·   ·   ·   ·

The old Church of St. Olave in Hart Street is one of decidedly nautical associations ; for not only did it contain formerly a special pew reserved for the use of the Navy Office in Seething Lane, but it has also—since the severance of the connexion with Deptford—been, so to speak, the parish of Trinity House, and thither the Master, Deputy Master, Elder and Younger Brethren repair on Trinity Monday in solemn state. It is rather a curious coincidence that St. Olave's should duplicate the cheerful skull-and-crossbones device of St. Nicholas at Deptford, over its churchyard gate— an emblem which one would think decidedly more appropriate in association with pirates than with pilots !

You go down two steps when you enter St. Olave's from the street, and the smoky little churchyard where the city sparrows twitter over the blackened gravestones is on a higher level than the street again, quite two or three above the church floor. It has been so since the days of the Great Plague, when three hundred and twenty-six people were buried there between July 4 and December 5, 1665.

" I presently into the church," Pepys writes, " the first time since I left London for the Plague ;

and it frightened me indeed to go though the church, more than I thought it could have done, to see so many graves lie so high upon the churchyard where people have been buried of the plague. I was much troubled at it, and do not think to go through it again a good while."

There are several interesting things to be seen in the church, which is one of the six or seven which escaped the Great Fire. There is a handsome carved pulpit which is either Grinling Gibbons's own work or that of a pupil, whence no doubt Mr. Pepys heard and nodded asleep over many of those " dull, tiresome sermons " he mentioned so frequently. There are effigies of beruffed and befarthingaled knights and ladies. There is the epitaph of a chairman of the East India Company and the Turkey Company. And underneath the tower there is a modest inscription which records how " John Hynlond, Senior and Skyner of London, in his life tyme being of the age of fourscore and seven yeares dyd give Forty shillinges yearlie to be bestoed in New Castell Cole for the relief of the Poore of this Parish."

" New Castell Cole "—what a picture those three words call up of the days when the sailing colliers used to come crowding up London River, "backing and filling " with the tide as their custom was, with their top-hatted skippers smoking and spitting over the rail !

mutton ; and after it a fearsome mess, into which the skipper poked an inquiring fork.

" What div ye ca' this, cook ? " he asked, scratching his head.

" Yon's yer goose," said the cook proudly. " Ah've postponed it for ye ! "

But for all their roughness, their lack of education, and their occasional drunkenness and brutality, these old collier skippers and crews were fine seamen. The coasts they sailed were among the most dangerous, the waters in which they earned their daily bread among the most stormy and wintry in the whole world. Book learning they had none, but of weather lore, handed down from father to son through generations of seafarers, they had a bountiful store. And their ships were as splendid a type of small craft as has ever been evolved to meet the needs of a special trade. They were built to stand hard weather and killing cargoes, and they were built to last. And last they did. There are instances recorded of these old brigs still going strong when they were well over a century old.

It was in the Geordies that many a great seaman learned his trade in days gone by—chief among them being, of course, Captain Cook, whose experience had taught him to think so highly of the craft in which he had his early training that he recommended the purchase of a Whitby collier for the purpose of his later voyages of discovery.

But they are gone now, the stout little ships, the hard old skippers—gone like many another such trade within the last fifty years or so. Where are the billyboys and ketches from the East Coast which used to come down from Sunderland with cargoes of bottles? I saw a ketch unloading a cargo of glass bottles in the docks not long ago. But she hailed from Amsterdam, and her bottles, I rather think, from Germany.

CHAPTER XIII

SOME OLD HOUSE FLAGS

The Virtue of Bunting—An Interesting Collection—Blackwall Flags—The China Fleet—The Wool Clippers—Clyde Fourposters —A Pacific Coast Memory—The Return of the Windjammer.

THERE is a wonderful virtue in good bunting. It has about it something so wholly genuine and honest, like oak and teak and hemp rope—the harsh homely feel of it, its good wholesome colours, its way of wearing to the last rag and shred. It pretends to be nothing other than it is, and that is a rare quality in times like these. And it is one of the few things in Ship Alley that does not vanish altogether or change beyond recognition with the years.

There is still bunting to flutter over the tops of the warehouses, though yards and sails be gone, still house flags and ensigns and the pleasant gay colours of the International Signal Code in the flag lockers of modern cargo steamers, still the old heartening sight of the Blue Peter fluttering down from the fore-truck of the outward bound. Is there, I wonder, anyone who is not to some degree respon-

sive to the thrill of that moment ? Not I, for
one ; and on the day when I find myself so I think
I shall be done with dock-haunting for ever.

I suppose there is nowhere a more interesting
collection of bunting than that which is stowed away
in chests in the Poplar Public Library, and only
sees the light on special occasions, such as corona-
tions and shipping exhibitions.   There are preserved
the house flags of very many of the famous shipping
firms of days gone by—owners of those fleets of
fast and sightly ships which did so much to build
up the commercial greatness of Britain, and which
have in many cases passed into oblivion with so
amazing and so sudden a completeness.   They are
mostly flags which have some connexion with
London ; and that—so far as the tea and the wool
trade of last century went—meant practically all.
And many of them are the actual ones which once
floated at the main-truck of ships whose names
were household words to an elder generation of
seafarers.

They speak of a tradition of loyalty, of ungrudging
service, of esprit de corps, which is growing all too
rare in this material age.   They were the merchant
seamen's regimental colour.   Their honour was his
honour while he served under them, as his ship's
honour was his ; and he would give his life if need
be to uphold it.   So you read of the crew of a
China clipper flying aloft in their shirt-tails to shake

the reefs out lest a rival should pass her, or bringing their blankets out and spreading them in the rigging that no least breath of a favourable wind might be wasted. It was a devotion not always, it may be, generously or even justly rewarded. But the man who has never known what it is to give himself for a cause has missed a good deal of the best in life. And if he is going to govern his actions on the principle of " I ain't goin' to bust myself. No bloody fear ! " it is not the master alone who is the loser.

Here are to be seen the flags of the old East India Company and of its successors—of the great Blackwall firms of Money Wigram and R. & H. Green, the former with the central blue patch over the St. George's Cross, the latter with the cross uppermost. Money Wigram's flag is still in existence as that of the Federal Steam Navigation Company ; Green's is as extinct as the ships that sailed under it. Those ships were the aristocracy of the sea — Wigram's " Kent," " Essex," " True Briton," and " Southampton," Green's " Newcastle," " Agincourt," " Alfred," and " Anglesey," were the perfection of British shipbuilding in the days of oak and teak, and never were ships better officered or better manned.

The blue cross on a white ground was the device of that celebrated Tyneside firm, T. & W. Smith, whose ships were so well known in the ports of

Madras and Calcutta before steam and the Suez
Canal drove them from the seas. The " Marl-
borough " and " Blenheim," built in their own
yard at Newcastle, were the pride of the fleet.
They are a name and a memory—no more.

The Scottish lion ramps in ruddy gold beneath
the motto " Sub Spe " on the flag of Duncan Dunbar,
the story of whose ships is told elsewhere in this
volume, as also that of Joseph Somes's fleet, which
flew the St. George's cross and gold anchor.

The red swallow-tail flag with the black ball
will be recognised at once as that associated with the
magnificent clipper ships " James Baines," " Lightning," and " Donald Mackay." The other red
swallow-tail flag with the well-known six-pointed
star, so familiar to our own time in connexion with
the White Star Line's mail steamers, has an interesting history. It was originally the property of
Messrs. Pilkington & Wilson, of Liverpool, and
by them was flown on such famous ships as
" Red Jacket," " White Star," " Shalimar," and
" Chariot of Fame," both flag and name being
acquired from Messrs. Pilkington & Wilson when
they retired from business by Mr. T. H. Ismay, the
founder of the present White Star Line.

And, speaking of black balls, there is another
black ball device in this collection. It is, strictly
speaking, not a flag at all, being merely a black
circle which used to be hoisted at the main instead

12

of a flag in the ships of Messrs. John Blyth & Co. Their ships traded to the West Indies with sugar, and owing to their yellow paint were always called the " pea-soup frigates."

Here, too, are the flags of the China tea fleet— MacCunn's " flying horse," renowned for its association with the wonderful " Sir Lancelot," the ship which under her famous skipper (Robinson) made such marvellous passages from Shanghai and Foochow in the heyday of the tea trade. She was owned by an Arab in her later days, and, though it may sound a come-down, he used her well. She was one of the sights of Calcutta for several years, and apprentices can remember being taken on board her that they might see one of the finest specimens of British shipbuilding. She weathered more than one Indian Ocean cyclone, but at last one took her and her whole company to the bottom together. Shaw Maxton's red flag with the white and blue diamond calls to mind those fairy ships with fairy names, " Ariel," " Oberon," and " Titania." Who knows not the story of " Ariel's " great race with " Taeping " and " Scrica," when the three ships docked on the same tide ? There is a thrill in it still. " Titania " was one of the last survivors of the tea fleet. She was owned in her old age—alas, that a fairy queen should ever grow old !—by the Hudson Bay Company, and, dainty yacht-like little vessel though she was, she could

hold her own and more against the big Cape
Horners of the 'nineties.

Fifty years ago no flag was better known wherever
ships could sail than the blue flag with the St.
Patrick's cross on white. That was the house
flag of John Willis—" Captain John," that tough
old nut of whom so many tales are told, who had so
wonderful an eye for a good ship, and (be it added)
a good bargain. Willis owned more than one famous
ship—" The Tweed," " Hallowe'en," " Blackadder "
—but to most people he is the man who owned
" Cutty Sark," that evergreen veteran who seems
to renew herself perpetually at some secret fount
of youth, like a sort of feminine marine Antæus,
drawing continual strength from the sea as he from
the earth.

Then there are the flags of the wool fleet—the
Aberdeen six-pointed star of Messrs. George
Thompson's fleet, which still flies on their smart
steamers between London and Australia, the
successors of the beautiful sailing fleet which was
the pride of Circular Quay and Sandridge Pier
forty years ago. " Thermopylae," " Salamis,"
" Star of Peace," " Jerusalem "—the names are
worthy of the stately ships that bore them. I
think there are now none of them left. The
" Pericles," one of the last, went to the knacker a
year or two ago.

Carmichael's golden fleece on a blue ground

13

backed by the white St. Andrew's cross—this is the very flag which was flown by the beautiful " Mermerus," one of a whole galaxy of lovely sisters named after kings and heroes and watery gods. " Glaucus," " Thessalus," " Medea," " Argonaut," " Aeolus," " Talus "—they are all gone but, perhaps, " Argonaut," which, with a sister ship, " Argo," is (or was quite lately) owned in Norway as the " Seileren."

Duthie's hand and dagger calls to mind that great little ship, the " Ann Duthie," one of the few which can claim to have got the better of the " Cutty Sark." The " Brilliant " was another famous little Duthie clipper in the wool trade. She and the " Pericles " were great rivals. And the " Port Jackson," too, made her early voyages under the Duthie flag, before her Devitt & Moore period as a cadet ship.

Devitt & Moore's red and blue with the white centre was another which flew over some fine vessels. Their " Rodney " was a very fast sailer ; both she and the same firm's " City of Adelaide" were among the " Cutty Sark's " serious rivals. The " Sobraon " was the pride of the fleet, and several of the Dunbar ships were also included in it after old Dunbar died.

Gone are the Glasgow Lochs, hard-driven ships and big passage-makers to the Colonies—gone like the shadow of a dream. Gone are Corry's Irish Stars

which sailed under the red heart on a white
ground.   Great ships in their time. . . . The " Star
of Italy " went out to Australia in seventy-eight
days, and the " Star of France " made a fine race
of it with Beazley's " John o' Gaunt " somewhere in
the 'eighties. Some few of them survive in the
Alaska Packers' fleet. They make one voyage a
year north from 'Frisco to bring in the salmon
pack from Alaska.

Rose, of Aberdeen, is the last of all the great
owners in the Australian trade to fly his flag over a
wool clipper. His " Mount Stewart " has survived
the shipping slump which followed the war boom,
and is still sailing to the nitrate ports under the
Red Duster.

. . . . .

And now we come to the first big fleets of Clyde
and Liverpool " four-posters " which sailed in the
Frisco grain fleet and later in the West Coast
trade—the ships which saw the last of the sail-
trained apprentice.

The sailing ship had passed her zenith in their
day. " Floating warehouses," so old sailormen
called them who looked back with regret to the
clipper ships. They were built for capacity, not
speed. They were often cruelly undermanned,
sometimes mercilessly overloaded. But something
of grace and beauty was theirs still : the beauty of

14

mighty yards, of the fine mesh of rigging against the sky, of canvas, furled or spread, of scoured planking, of glossy teak. In them the seaman was still a seaman ; and indeed it is doubtful if the sea ever asked of those who follow her a greater toll of endurance, of skill and of courage than that which was paid by the men who sailed in the Cape Horn trade in the days of the decline of the windjammer.

Law's Scottish Shires, whose flag is in the collection, were among the best of them. I used to know their " Kinross-shire " in Victoria, some ten or twelve years ago. She was a fine ship, with painted ports like all Law's fleet ; and I remember well watching her towing out one morning towards Cape Flattery, and thinking of the time she would have off the Horn, with a deck-load of lumber up to her topgallant rail. Still, she got home all right, and lasted the war out, only to go missing at the finish in the North Atlantic, under the Norwegian flag and the new name of " Fiorino." I smell lumber again when I think of her ; and I hear the scream of the saws, and see the turbaned Hindoos with their carts loading mill-wood. I wonder what became of her dog when she was sold foreign. He was as much a part of her as her own jibboom, for he never went ashore. He was an old dog, though, so perhaps he died under the Duster.

Hughes-Jones's old Liverpool ship " Celtic Monarch " has had many ups and downs since sh sailed under their flag. She was dismasted in the Pacific in 1910, and was then converted into a hulk. But the war gave her a new lease of life, as it did to many of her kind.

Then when peace came she was again turned into a hulk. But that was not to be the end of her.

'Frisco is to have her windjammers again. Once again it is to be

> Blow, bullies, blow,
> For Califor-ni-o,

as it was when the Yankee clippers came roaring westward by the long sea road with their tough-nut skippers and their hard-fisted mates in the days of the Forty-nine gold rush, and down to the time when the 'Frisco grain fleet gathered together the last of the splendour of sail.

For years the famous harbour has been all but deserted by the tall beauties of the sea. And now Mr. James D. Rolph, mayor of the city, has inaugurated a regular service of sailing vessels between California and the Far East. Four ships form the nucleus of the venture, and the number will be added to should it prove successful.

Of the four, one is a wooden barquentine built in America during the war. The others are much more interesting, both as ships and by reason of their history.

The " Annie M. Reid " was formerly the " Howard
D. Troop." She sounds like a hard nut if she isn't
one. Those benevolent-sounding names, that sound
like old gentlemen in white waistcoats, generally used
to indicate a Down-east mate with a face like a
chunk of wood and a fist like a fivefold block, which
he didn't hesitate to use by way of emphasizing his
remarks. But she could sail. She once made the
passage from Sydney to Falmouth with grain in
eighty-two days—and grain, be it remembered, is
a very different proposition from the wool with
which most of the crack runs from Australia were
made.

Then there is the " Golden Gate," also an
ex-British ship ; the " Lord Shaftesbury," which
has loaded grain under that name many a time at
'Frisco ; and lastly this old " Celtic Monarch,"
whose flag is in Poplar Library.

CHAPTER XIV

LAID UP

The old " Harmony "—From Whaler to Mission Ship—The Shipkeeper—A Vanishing Type—Mike and the Pig—Memories.

THE London Docks during the winter and spring wouldn't seem quite complete without the masts and yards of the old " Harmony " lending a welcome touch of picturesqueness to the quiet corner of the Hermitage Basin, where she makes her winter quarters.

She is not at all a bad little ship to look at in a homely fashion—nothing of the clipper about her, but her lines are good, and she has a pretty little figurehead of a comely young woman of the conventional type. Her counter shows her name— " Harmony "—and her port of register, London.

She is a small barque-rigged auxiliary built of wood, and the sheathing about her cutwater suggests at once that her business is such as to bring her into close quarters with either the Arctic or the Antarctic floes.

A whaler—that is one's first thought, or would be if this were the Pacific coast. But—although

London was one of the chief ports for whalers in days gone by—a whaler sailing out of the modern Port of London would be decidedly an anachronism. Nevertheless, a whaler the little ship has been in her time, for she has a history which is both long and interesting.

When she was built some sixty years ago she was engaged in the East Indian tea trade. In those days she was called " Lorna Doone," and the damsel of the figurehead is no doubt a representation of Blackmore's heroine. Probably, if the name is anything to go by, she was west-country owned and built.

Later on she passed to a Dundee firm, and sailed as a whaler out of that port for many years. Last of all she was acquired by her present owners, the Moravian Mission, for the purposes of their work in Labrador, in which business she has been sailing ever since.

Every summer she makes a voyage to the far North with general cargo—tinned foods, tools, clothing, medical requisites—in fact, everything you can think of—which is bartered with the Labrador Eskimo for sealskins, whale-oil, furs, and suchlike commodities. She visits the lonely missionary posts in the Labrador wilds, and takes out missionaries to take the places of those whose leave is falling due. Recently she brought one home who had been over thirty years in the country. She carries a

motor pinnace on the top of the deckhouse amidships, and this is used for navigating rivers where
the ship herself cannot go. During the short, hot
summer of Labrador she visits most parts of the
coast as far as St. John's, Newfoundland, remaining
in those waters until the approach of the freeze-up,
when she returns to her familiar corner in Hermitage
Basin until the following summer.

Built throughout of oak and teak, she is an
admirably seaworthy little ship, despite her small
size (she carries a cargo of about three hundred
tons). She can stand North Atlantic weather with
the best, riding like a cork the big seas which
sometimes give the Atlantic liners a dusting.

If old ships dream, this little " Harmony," *ex*
" Lorna Doone," must have plenty of material for
dreams in her long and varied career ; and if old
ships talk, she must have many a reminiscence to
exchange with the other ships in the peace and
quiet of Hermitage Basin, where the " China Ship "
just the other side of the dock wall recalls one phase
of her romantic past, when she knew warmth and
colour and the East instead of the mist and cold of
the North, and when—low be it whispered !—it
may even be that rough voices roared forth songs
which were most assuredly not hymns in that
stoutly built deckhouse which is now the missionaries' saloon.

.   .   .   .   .

The old shipkeeper who looks after her has just finished his pottering about for the day, and is leaning over the rail with his pipe in his mouth. It is something of a paradox that smoking is strictly forbidden all over the docks, but on board a ship in the docks you may smoke like a furnace.

He looks rather as if he wanted someone to yarn with. Solitude is one of the principal drawbacks of a shipkeeper's life—especially since most ship-keepers have arrived at that time of life when they are either surly or garrulous.

This old fellow must be one of the very few shipkeepers left around the docks nowadays. Times have changed. In the sailing ship days practically every ship had a shipkeeper, usually some wheezy old pensioner who had at last been reluctantly driven to the admission that he was too old to go to sea. Steamers don't need shipkeepers. There is generally someone, winchman or what not, left on board. And they seldom make a long stay in port, in these days of hurry and bustle : it is just a sharp turn round and out again.

But when a sailing vessel came in, and all her crew went roaring into Sailor Town with their pay to burn, the shipkeeper came into his kingdom, like a garrulous old phantom haunting the deserted forecastle and the forsaken cabins.

And queer old characters, too, some of them were ! There was one very well known old fellow, Mike

Donovan by name, who always used to have a shipkeeper's job in one or another of Nourse's fleet of coolie ships named after rivers—the " Foyle," " Erne," " Liffey," " Mersey," and so on. Many people, no doubt, will remember the " Mersey " when she was the White Star Line's cadet training ship. She is still afloat as the Norwegian " Dvergso."

Captain " Paddy " Nourse, like most shipowners of the old school, was a bit of an autocrat, and this old fellow Mike Donovan was one of the very few who didn't hold him in some degree of awe.

It chanced one Saturday that for some reason Mike's wages were not forthcoming. So off the old chap went to a German pork butcher in the Poplar High Street and sold the ship's pig, handing over the price of " Dennis " to Captain Nourse next time he put in an appearance, minus the amount of his own wages !

There is a story of one old skipper who was too mean to employ a shipkeeper. He used to live on board with his wife when the ship was in port, eating up the mouldy flour and weevily biscuits left over from the last voyage. When he died he left quite a nice little fortune behind him, and his wife—poor soul !—was so astonished that she went clean off her head and ended her days in a lunatic asylum.

Ah, well, there are very few shipkeepers' jobs

going nowadays! Perhaps if there were there would not be the men to fill them. It is a pity. It was a pleasant life for an old shellback broke by time or the sea. He was among ships. He could smell the old ship smells, hear the old talk of ports, of cargoes, of the sea. And now and then there would come an old shipmate to yarn with of the great ships and great days in the years when he was young. . . .

CHAPTER XV

LLOYD'S LIST

The World's Oldest Newspapers—The Power of a Name—
Vessels for Sale—Candle Auctions—Heart's Content.

IT is a favourite pastime with some people to
make lists of books which they would choose
to be their companions in case of their being
cast away upon an uninhabited island. For my
own part I doubt if I should have much heart for
literature under such circumstances—unless it were
a manual of boat-building ; and that without the
requisite tools would be like a tin of sardines without
an opener. To sit upon a desert island watching
for a ship would be bad : to sit there and read
Bacon's Essays would be, if anything, worse. What
beloved book under such conditions but would lose
its charm for ever ?

But if I were—not on an island, but at any rate
so situated that my periodical reading was limited
to two a day—then I rather think that one of the
two would be Lloyd's List, by which I mean not
what some people mean when they use the term
" Lloyd's List," quite incorrectly, to signify Lloyd's

Register, but that time-honoured institution which has been steadily recording the movements of shipping for nearly two hundred years.

Lloyd's List is—with the sole exception of the " London Gazette "—the oldest newspaper in existence. It started life, to be exact, in 1726, in a world which was actually very much smaller and relatively very much bigger than it is to-day ; when there was no Australia, no North Pacific coast, no Japan, so far as shipping was concerned, but when it still took the best part of a year to get to India, and America was not much less than a month distant. A son was not yet born to a humble family of the name of Cook in a Yorkshire cottage when that first " Lloyd's " was printed. Captain Jenkins was still in possession of both his ears. Anson's four years' voyage was not begun, nor the colony of Georgia founded, and Admiral Hosier was dying of grief and fever at Porto Bello.

It was no doubt but a small sheet in those days. It grew out of a list of arrivals and departures of ships provided for his patrons by the proprietor of the original Lloyd's Coffee House in Tower Street, a place much resorted to by merchants and captains. The first list to be printed began to come out in 1688, but it only ran a few months, and when the present one appeared for the first time Lloyd had been dead for some years.

And so it has gone on ever since, telling its tidings

of the sea—of the comings and goings of ships, of wrecks, of strandings, of fires, of the lost and the missing, of

> Ships dismasted, that were hailed
> And sent no answer back again. . . .

Those early issues would no doubt contain frequent announcements of ships " for sale by the candle," a method of auctioning ships which continued to be in use until comparatively recent times. There are, I believe, a few very old men who can recall its being practised.

The procedure was to light a piece of candle— generally about an inch long—which was enclosed in a horn case as a precaution against its untimely extinction either by accident or design. As soon as the candle was alight the bidding was open, and the ship fell to the last bid made before the candle's last expiring flicker. It must have been an exciting moment, when all eyes were fixed upon the sinking flame, and the eager bids came like the rattle of musketry as it leaped, expired, and leaped again.

They sell no ships by the candle now. But there are still interesting possibilities in the columns of " Vessels for Sale," lurking concealed among lists of self-trimming colliers and steel cargo steamers and dumb barges. If I want one thing less than a self-trimming collier it is a dumb barge. The eye is attracted for a moment by a schooner of 240 tons, a ketch of 130 tons, an auxiliary motor vessel. But hold, what have we here ? For sale at Newcastle —" a teak hulk, very strongly built, about 400 tons."

There is about that teak hulk something of the quality of an unsigned Old Master which *may* turn out to be a Titian. It doesn't say how old she is. Perhaps no one knows. Perhaps she is some ancient East Indiaman on her last legs that has been trudging the North Sea for years until she got too old to go to sea again. She must have been built out East ; and her small tonnage suggests that she is an old stager. She might quite conceivably be one of Joseph Somes's or Duncan Dunbar's early ships ; perhaps she might date back earlier still. Old wooden ships—especially old teak ships—hang together practically for ever, built, as they often were, three planks thick. They are as long-lived as donkeys or tortoises. The old " Java " and the " Three Brothers " are cases in point. The old " Betsy Cains," the " Cognac Packet," and the " Brotherly Love " were centenarians. The ketch " Good Intent " was going strong when she had passed her hundredth year. And that wonderful veteran, the " Truelove," was broken up when she was a hundred and nine years old, after a career surely as hard and as varied as any ship ever had.

I suppose it doesn't seem interesting to—well, to people who are not interested, which is perhaps not so banal an observation as it sounds. Some people are not even remotely interested in those columns of stocks and shares which others pore over like alchemists over their vials, and when their eyesight gives out have read aloud to them by their nieces until they totter into their graves. And there are, I believe, people who get wildly excited over those incomprehensible paragraphs which announce that " tapioca is quiet " or that " linseed is steady." What would happen if tapioca were noisy, or if linseed forsook the paths of sobriety, one shudders to contemplate !

One need not even have any material interest at stake to feel the fascination of a shipping paper. There is a certain sentimental ballad, much favoured by drawing-room singers, which (being paraphrased) states that if all the singer's ships were to come home at one and the same time there would not be a harbour in the world—no, not Sydney or Rio or Carrick Roads—big enough to hold 'em all at once. Well, of course no one would be such a fool as to have all his ships coming home at once ! But the point is that it is possible to be the spiritual possessor of just such a number of ships as that indicated in that otherwise rather unpractical song, without being subjected to what we are assured by those who have been through it is the extremely harassing business of owning them in the material sense.

I think it was old Captain John Willis who was once pottering about one of his ships when someone came up to him and asked if he were the captain.

" No," growled old Willis. " No such luck ! I'm the miserable owner ! "

Are they not in a sense yours, those ships you have known ? Are they not part of yourself, part of your being, part of that jumble of memories and hopes and regrets which is your life . . . so that to see their familiar names is like striking palms with an old friend across the gulf of the years ? How they bring back the old scenes, the old faces . . . the fair ships loved and lost, the ports half forgotten, the old shipmates' voices, the songs, the yarns, the laughter of long ago !

Great is the power of a name when it touches the hidden chords of memory, and no less, perhaps, when its magic is the magic of the strange skyline, the unadventured sea. There are names of old Spanish ports of the buccaneers, musical, slow and stately . . . Cienfuegos, Puerto Castilla, La Guayra . . . there are names with the sound of wind-chimed bells in them on temples of smiling Buddhas . . . the breaking of the surf on coral reefs . . . the thunder of the wind through the Baltic pine forests . . . strange names, savage names, kindly names . . . Mazatlan, Port au Prince, Heart's Content. . . .

Heart's Content—Heart's Content ! Did ever the imagination of man frame a fairer name ? Does it stand for some earthly paradise of the " still-vex'd Bermoothes," some coral-girt gem of the blue Southern Seas ? Not so. To each his own dream of Heart's Content, and to the man who named this one it was a few white houses, a little church, a rickety wharf on the wild and stormy shores of the Gulf of St. Lawrence.

That was Heart's Content to the fisherman of the Grand Banks ; and what, after all, could one ask better of life ?

A portion of labour that the sleep to come may be the sweeter . . . a portion of hardship that the comfort afterwards may be the more precious . . . a few risks taken, a few battles won with wind and sea . . . a prosperous voyage and a fair landfall . . . and a safe anchorage at the end of it in the port of Heart's Content. . . .

PRINTED BY
JARROLD AND SONS LTD.
NORWICH